Advent
Journal

DISCIPLE of CHRIST
EDUCATION IN VIRTUE

Mother of Life

Published by Lumen Ecclesiae Press
4101 East Joy Road
Ann Arbor, Michigan 48105

Editor: Sister John Dominic Rasmussen, O.P.
Cover Design: Amy Beers
Book Design Layout and Permissions: Linda Kelly
Copy Editor: Claudia Volkman

ISBN 978-0-9982607-8-5

Second Printing
Printed in the United States of America

Requests for permission to make copies of any part of the work should be directed to: educationinvirtue.com

Table of Contents

Introduction..4

Preparation for Advent...6

Lectio Divina...8

Sunday Readings/Feast Days..68

LIVING AS A DISCIPLE OF CHRIST..............................74

     Conversion...78

     Prayer...86

     Virtue...92

     Gift of Self...96

     Learn–Live–Witness...98

Living Advent with the Word

"Meditation engages thought, imagination, emotion, and desire. This mobilization of faculties is necessary in order to deepen our convictions of faith, prompt the conversion of our hearts, and strengthen our will to follow Christ."
(CCC, 2708)

As you open your mind and heart to the Holy Spirit and encounter the Word of God, you will begin to experience a renewed faith and a closer relationship with the Person of Jesus Christ. The questions are written to guide your prayerful reading of Scripture and assist you in understanding the passage. They are not intended to be questions to complete for an assignment but more of a means for you to establish a relationship with Jesus.

✝ In a spirit of recollection, place yourself in God's presence.

✝ Recite a prayer: *Lord Jesus Christ, Son of the Living God, have mercy on me, a sinner.*

✝ Daily read the Scripture verses and follow the steps for *Lectio Divina.* Let the Word of God penetrate your mind and heart and ponder the Word throughout the course of the day.

Preparing the Manger of Our Hearts

In the season of Advent, we join with Mary in preparing the manger of our hearts to receive the Christ Child. By actively practicing the virtues, we seek to adopt the attitude of expectancy that Mary and the Chosen People of Israel had as they waited in joyful hope for the coming of the Messiah. In imitation of her receptivity to God's grace and the transforming power of His presence, we seek an openness to the Holy Spirit's action in bringing to perfection our fallen human nature. The practices are suggestions on how to actively live the Word in order to be a more faithful disciple.

My Meditation

Throughout the Advent season "My Meditation" is a place for you to journal about your encounter with the Person of Jesus Christ.

Wreath

A wreath of greenery with three purple candles and one pink

Green branches — God promises everlasting life
Circle — God has no beginning and no end
Purple candles — royalty and penance
Pink candle — joy

Christ Candle

A large white candle decorated with a Chi Rho

White — innocence and purity
Flame — Jesus is the light of the world

Jesse Tree

A branch or tree decorated with symbols tracing Jesus' heritage and ancestry

We unite ourselves with the people of the Old Testament in waiting for the birth of Christ while also looking towards His second coming. Our desire should be to allow Him to transform us more completely into His own image and likeness present within us.

Date	Event/Person	Scripture	Symbol
Dec. 1	Adam and Eve	Genesis 3:1–24	Apple
Dec. 2	Noah and the flood	Genesis 6, 7, 8:1–9	Ark
Dec. 3	God's promise to Noah	Genesis 9:8–17	Rainbow
Dec. 4	God's covenant with Abraham	Genesis 12:1–3; 18:1–5	Stars (representing his descendants)
Dec. 5	Abraham's sacrifice	Genesis 22:1–18	Ram and altar
Dec. 6	Jacob's dream	Genesis 28:10–22	Ladder
Dec. 7	Joseph saves Israel	Genesis 37–45 (all)	Coat of many colors
Dec. 8	God calls Moses	Exodus 2:23–4:20	Burning bush
Dec. 9	God feeds His people	Exodus 16:1–36	Manna and quail
Dec. 10	God gives Moses His laws	Exodus 19–20:1–2	Stone tablets
Dec. 11	Wall of Jericho falls	Joshua 6:1–20	Horns
Dec. 12	Ruth helps Naomi	Ruth 1–4	Bushel of wheat
Dec. 13	God calls Samuel	1 Samuel 3:1–21	Boy sleeping
Dec. 14	Jesse's family is chosen	1 Samuel 16:1–13 (Isaiah 11:1)	Branch growing from stump
Dec. 15	David kills Goliath	1 Samuel 17:1–54	Sling and stone
Dec. 16	Solomon's wisdom	1 Kings 3:3–28	Light (torch)
Dec. 17	God takes Elijah to heaven	2 Kings 2:1–13	Chariot of fire
Dec. 18	Daniel in the lion's den	Daniel 6:1–28	Lion
Dec. 19	Jonah in the whale	Jonah 1 and 2	Whale
Dec. 20	The Blessed Virgin Mary	Matthew 1:23 and Isaiah 7:14	White Rose
Dec. 21	Gabriel appears to Mary	Luke 1:26–38	Angel
Dec. 22	St. Joseph	Matthew 1:18–25	Carpenter's tool
Dec. 23	Mary and Joseph travel to Bethlehem	Luke 2:1–5	Mary and Joseph on donkey
Dec. 24	Wise Men follow the star	Matthew 2:1–12	Star

Through our faith, hope, and love he wants his light to shine over and over again in the night of the world… That night is "today" whenever the "Word" again becomes "flesh" or genuine human reality. "The Christ child comes" in a real sense whenever human beings act out of authentic love for the Lord. —Joseph Ratzinger, *Dogma and Preaching: Applying Christian Doctrine to Daily Life* (San Francisco: Ignatius Press, 2011).

The word "Advent" can be translated as "coming" or "presence" in Latin. Through Mary, Christ, the Son of God, has come into the world. As a baptized Christian, you are called to bring Christ to others. The following questions will assist you in preparing for the season of Advent.

During the season of Advent, what ways can you be a light of God's presence to others?

_____

_____

_____

_____

Review the list of Advent virtues on the next page and decide which ones you will seek to cultivate this season. Write down the virtues and refer to them during the Advent season.

_____

_____

_____

_____

Spend a few moments in silence asking Jesus to show you how you need to prepare the manger of your heart. Write down what He says to you.

_____

_____

_____

_____

_____

Advent Virtues

VIRTUE	KNOWING THE VIRTUE	LIVING THE VIRTUE	SCRIPTURE CONNECTION
Prayerfulness	Being still, listening, and being willing to talk to God as a friend	• Making personal visits to the Blessed Sacrament • Taking initiative to pray • Practicing recollection	"Mary kept all these things, reflecting on the in her heart." *(Luke 2:19)*
Humility	Awareness that all our gifts come from God and appreciation of the gifts of others	• Acknowledging the talents of others by praising them • Saying "thank you" when praised for an action well done	"And Mary said, 'My soul proclaims the greatness of the Lord." *(Luke 1:46)*
Obedience	Assenting to rightful authority without hesitation or resistance	• Honoring your teachers and parents by doing what they ask • Anticipating their requests and wants • Smiling while doing a task you should do	"When Joseph awoke, he did as the angel of the Lord had commanded him and took his wife into his home." *(Matthew 1:24)*
Generosity	Giving of oneself in a willing and cheerful manner for the good of others	• Willingly helping others • Freely giving of your time and gifts	"For God so loved the world that he gave his only Son..." *(John 3:16)*
Gratitude	Thankful disposition of mind and heart	• Expressing thanks by words or deeds and in your prayers	"The Mighty One has done great things for me, and holy is his name." *(Luke 1:49)*
Patience	Bearing present difficulties calmly	• Waiting for your turn • Listening while others are speaking • Remaining calm when you don't get what you want	"...And Joseph too went up from Galilee from the town of Nazareth to Judea, to the city of David that is called Bethlehem..." *(Luke 2:1–7)*
Docility	Willingness to be taught	• Willingness to listen to directions • Listening to and thinking about another person's idea	"When the angels went away to heaven the shepherds said to one another, "Let us go, then, to Bethlehem..." *(Luke 2:15)*

> "I would like in particular to recall and recommend the ancient tradition of Lectio Divina: the diligent reading of Sacred Scripture accompanied by prayer brings about that intimate dialogue in which the person reading hears God who is speaking, and in praying, responds to him with trusting openness of heart (cf. Dei Verbum, n.25) If it is effectively promoted, this practice will bring to the Church – I am convinced of it – a new spiritual springtime."
> — Pope Benedict XVI

 Jesus Christ said, "Learn from me" (Matthew 11:49) and offered his life as a model for us. To be a disciple of Christ means we seek to learn from Him on how to live as His disciple. Through reading and meditating on the Word of God, we come to know Him and develop a personal relationship with Him.

READING (*LECTIO*)

What does the Word of God say?
    Read slowly, listening attentively to the Word of God.

MEDITATION (*MEDITATIO*)

What does the Word of God say to me?
    Spend time with the word or phrase that touched your heart.

PRAYER (*ORATIO*)

What do I say to the Lord in response to His Word?
    Let the word or phrase shape your response to God, such as praise, petition, thanksgiving.

CONTEMPLATION (CONTEMPLATIO)

What conversion of mind, heart, and life is the Lord asking of me?
    Rest in His presence, and open your heart to receive His Love.

ACTION (ACTIO)

How has encountering God's love in His Word changed me? How can my life be a gift to others?
    Ask the Lord to show you where to grow in virtue.

Mary was the first person to experience *Lectio Divina* as she pondered all the events of Christ's life (Luke 2:19).

> *Matthew 8:5–11*
>
> When Jesus entered Capernaum, a centurion approached him and appealed to him, saying, "Lord, my servant is lying at home paralyzed, suffering dreadfully." He said to him, "I will come and cure him." The centurion said in reply, "Lord, I am not worthy to have you enter under my roof; only say the word and my servant will be healed. For I too am a man subject to authority, with soldiers subject to me. And I say to one, 'Go,' and he goes; and to another, 'Come here,' and he comes; and to my slave, 'Do this,' and he does it." When Jesus heard this, he was amazed and said to those following him, "Amen, I say to you, in no one in Israel have I found such faith. I say to you, many will come from the east and the west, and will recline with Abraham, Isaac, and Jacob at the banquet in the kingdom of heaven."

God's Word strikes the heart. What word or phrase touched your heart?

_____

_____

The centurion is a military officer who commanded one hundred men. How is his response to Jesus an example of faith?

_____

_____

The words of the centurion are recited before receiving Holy Communion. How does the reception of Holy Communion bring healing?

_____

_____

_____

Ask this question in prayer: "Jesus, show me how my faith can increase to believe and trust in Your healing power." Write down what He says to you.

_____

_____

_____

PRAYERFULNESS

Being still, listening, and being willing to talk to God as a friend

Prayer can truly change your life. For it turns your attention away from yourself and directs your mind and your heart toward the Lord. If we look only at ourselves, with our own limitations and sins, we quickly give way to sadness and discouragement. But if we keep our eyes fixed on the Lord, then our hearts are filled with hope, our minds are washed in the light of truth, and we come to know the fullness of the Gospel with all its promise and life. —St. Pope John Paul II

But when you pray, go to your inner room, close the door, and pray to your Father in secret. And your Father who sees in secret will repay you.
—Matthew 6:6

LISTENING	BEING STILL	INTERCESSION
SILENCE	ADORE	PRAISE

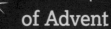
> ### Luke 10:21–24
>
> Jesus rejoiced in the Holy Spirit and said, "I give you praise, Father, Lord of heaven and earth, for although you have hidden these things from the wise and the learned you have revealed them to the childlike. Yes, Father, such has been your gracious will. All things have been handed over to me by my Father. No one knows who the Son is except the Father, and who the Father is except the Son and anyone to whom the Son wishes to reveal him."
>
> Turning to the disciples in private he said, "Blessed are the eyes that see what you see. For I say to you, many prophets and kings desired to see what you see, but did not see it, and to hear what you hear, but did not hear it."

God's Word strikes the heart. What word or phrase touched your heart?

_____

_____

Review the virtues on pages 93–95. Select three virtues that describe those who are childlike. Why do you think the mysteries of the kingdom are revealed to those who are childlike?

_____

_____

_____

Ask this question in prayer: "Father, Lord of heaven and earth, what do I need to change to see You and to be open to all You have revealed in Jesus?" Write down what He says to you.

_____

_____

_____

— Preparing the Manger of Your Heart —

"Blessed are the clean of heart, for they will see God." (Matthew 5:8)

Repeat the verse several times.

What keeps your heart from seeing God? Ask Him to cleanse your heart.

✳ My Meditation

Matthew 15:29–37

At that time: Jesus walked by the Sea of Galilee, went up on the mountain, and sat down there. Great crowds came to him, having with them the lame, the blind, the deformed, the mute, and many others. They placed them at his feet, and he cured them. The crowds were amazed when they saw the mute speaking, the deformed made whole, the lame walking, and the blind able to see, and they glorified the God of Israel.

Jesus summoned his disciples and said, "My heart is moved with pity for the crowd, for they have been with me now for three days and have nothing to eat. I do not want to send them away hungry, for fear they may collapse on the way." The disciples said to him, "Where could we ever get enough bread in this deserted place to satisfy such a crowd?" Jesus said to them, "How many loaves do you have?" "Seven," they replied, "and a few fish." He ordered the crowd to sit down on the ground. Then he took the seven loaves and the fish, gave thanks, broke the loaves, and gave them to the disciples, who in turn gave them to the crowds. They all ate and were satisfied. They picked up the fragments left over—seven baskets full.

God's Word strikes the heart. What word or phrase touched your heart?

_____

_____

How does Jesus show His tenderness and compassion toward the crowds?

_____

_____

Jesus felt pity when He saw the crowd of people without food, and He also felt pity when John the Baptist died. Write a prayer as if Jesus were talking to you in those times when you have felt sadness or were tired.

_____

_____

_____

_____

_____

Humility is an awareness that all one's gifts come from God and appreciation for the gifts of others. Ask Jesus to show you one of your gifts or talents that you can offer to Him. Write down what He says to you.

_____

_____

_____

_____

— Preparing the Manger of Your Heart —

Praise and thank God for your gifts and talents.
Ask Him to multiply them.

Matthew 7:21, 24–27

Jesus said to his disciples: "Not everyone who says to me, 'Lord, Lord,' will enter the kingdom of heaven, but only the one who does the will of my Father in heaven.

"Everyone who listens to these words of mine and acts on them will be like a wise man who built his house on rock. The rain fell, the floods came, and the winds blew and buffeted the house. But it did not collapse; it had been set solidly on rock. And everyone who listens to these words of mine but does not act on them will be like a fool who built his house on sand. The rain fell, the floods came, and the winds blew and buffeted the house. And it collapsed and was completely ruined."

God's Word strikes the heart. What word or phrase touched your heart?

_____

_____

Jesus gives this teaching to His disciples at the conclusion of the Sermon on the Mount (Matthew 5–7). What are some ways you can build your "house" on rock ("house" meaning your soul)?

_____

_____

_____

Mary is the perfect model of one who listened to the Word of God and acted upon it. What virtue(s) do you see in Mary? How did she act upon God's Word?

_____

_____

_____

_____

_____

Ask this question in prayer: "Jesus, Your mother listened to the Word and pondered the meaning. How can I change to be more open to the will of Your heavenly Father?" Write down what He says to you.

_____

_____

_____

_____

— Preparing the Manger of Your Heart —

**Disconnect completely and sit in silence with the Lord.
Listen with your heart to hear what He says to you.**

Matthew 9:27–31

As Jesus passed by, two blind men followed him, crying out, "Son of David, have pity on us!" When he entered the house, the blind men approached him and Jesus said to them, "Do you believe that I can do this?" "Yes, Lord," they said to him. Then he touched their eyes and said, "Let it be done for you according to your faith." And their eyes were opened. Jesus warned them sternly, "See that no one knows about this." But they went out and spread word of him through all that land.

God's Word strikes the heart. What word or phrase touched your heart?

_____

_____

The blind men knew it was Jesus and cried out, "Son of David, have pity on us." How were they able to see Jesus before being cured?

_____

_____

_____

Ask Jesus to show you the blind spots in your life, the sins which prevent you from seeing Him. Write down what He says to you.

_____

_____

_____

— Preparing the Manger of Your Heart —

Spend five to ten minutes in quiet prayer.

✦ My Meditation

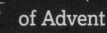

Matthew 9:35–10:1, 5A, 6–8

Jesus went around to all the towns and villages, teaching in their synagogues, proclaiming the gospel of the kingdom, and curing every disease and illness. At the sight of the crowds, his heart was moved with pity for them because they were troubled and abandoned, like sheep without a shepherd. Then he said to his disciples, "The harvest is abundant but the laborers are few; so ask the master of the harvest to send out laborers for his harvest."

Then he summoned his twelve disciples and gave them authority over unclean spirits to drive them out and to cure every disease and every illness.

Jesus sent out these twelve after instructing them thus, "Go to the lost sheep of the house of Israel. As you go, make this proclamation: 'The kingdom of heaven is at hand.' Cure the sick, raise the dead, cleanse lepers, drive out demons. Without cost you have received; without cost you are to give."

God's Word strikes the heart. What word or phrase touched your heart?

_____

_____

At the sight of the crowds, Jesus' heart was moved with pity (compassion). Describe the actions of Jesus.

_____

_____

_____

_____

What authority did Jesus give to the twelve disciples?

_____

Ask this question in prayer: "Jesus, is there someone in my life who is a "lost sheep"? Show me what I can do to bring the good news to that person." Write down what He says to you.

_____

_____

_____

— Preparing the Manger of Your Heart —

Have you considered being a priest or religious or do you know of someone who may be called to the priesthood or religious life? How can you encourage them to follow Jesus?

From a Homily in Praise of the Virgin Mother
The Whole World Awaits Mary's Reply

You have heard, O Virgin, that you will conceive and bear a son; you have heard that it will not be by man but by the Holy Spirit. The angel awaits an answer; it is time for him to return to God who sent him. We too are waiting, O Lady, for your word of compassion; the sentence of condemnation weighs heavily upon us.

The price of our salvation is offered to you. We shall be set free at once if you consent. In the eternal Word of God we all came to be, and behold, we die. In your brief response we are to be remade in order to be recalled to life. Tearful Adam with his sorrowing family begs this of you, O loving Virgin, in their exile from Paradise. Abraham begs it, David begs it. All the other holy patriarchs, your ancestors, ask it of you, as they dwell in the country of the shadow of death. This is what the whole earth waits for, prostrate at your feet. It is right in doing so, for on your word depends comfort for the wretched, ransom for the captive, freedom for the condemned, indeed, salvation for all the sons of Adam, the whole of your race.

Answer quickly, O Virgin. Reply in haste to the angel, or rather through the angel to the Lord. Answer with a word, receive the Word of God. Speak your own word, conceive the divine Word. Breathe a passing word, embrace the eternal Word.

Why do you delay, why are you afraid? Believe, give praise, and receive. Let humility be bold, let modesty be confident. This is no time for virginal simplicity to forget prudence. In this matter alone, O prudent Virgin, do not fear to be presumptuous. Though modest silence is pleasing, dutiful speech is now more necessary. Open your heart to faith, O blessed Virgin, your lips to praise, your womb to the Creator. See, the desired of all nations is at your door, knocking to enter. If he should pass by because of your delay, in sorrow you would begin to seek him afresh, the One whom your soul loves. Arise, hasten, open. Arise in faith, hasten in devotion, open in praise and thanksgiving. Behold the handmaid of the Lord, she says, be it done to me according to your word.

By Saint Bernard, Abbot

One day as Jesus was teaching, Pharisees and teachers of the law, who had come from every village of Galilee and Judea and Jerusalem, were sitting there, and the power of the Lord was with him for healing. And some men brought on a stretcher a man who was paralyzed; they were trying to bring him in and set him in his presence. But not finding a way to bring him in because of the crowd, they went up on the roof and lowered him on the stretcher through the tiles into the middle in front of Jesus. When Jesus saw their faith, he said, "As for you, your sins are forgiven." Then the scribes and Pharisees began to ask themselves, "Who is this who speaks blasphemies? Who but God alone can forgive sins?" Jesus knew their thoughts and said to them in reply, "What are you thinking in your hearts? Which is easier, to say, 'Your sins are forgiven,' or to say, 'Rise and walk'? But that you may know that the Son of Man has authority on earth to forgive sins"—he said to the one who was paralyzed, "I say to you, rise, pick up your stretcher, and go home." He stood up immediately before them, picked up what he had been lying on, and went home, glorifying God. Then astonishment seized them all and they glorified God, and, struck with awe, they said, "We have seen incredible things today."

God's Word strikes the heart. What word or phrase touched your heart?

_____

_____

Describe what the four men did to bring the paralytic to Jesus. What did Jesus see in these men?

_____

_____

Jesus knew their thoughts. How and why did He show that He is the Son of Man?

_____

_____

_____

The men who carried the paralytic exemplified the virtue of perseverance and the beauty of friendship. Imagine having a friend who is "paralyzed" in his faith and is not willing to pray or walk into a church. Write down what you would say to convince him or her to go to Jesus for healing.

_____

_____

_____

— Preparing the Manger of Your Heart —

Jesus knows your thoughts—surrender to Him the fears which "paralyze" your commitment to be a disciple of Christ.

What is one fear that prevents you from being a disciple?

Matthew 18:12–14

Jesus said to his disciples: "What is your opinion? If a man has a hundred sheep and one of them goes astray, will he not leave the ninety-nine in the hills and go in search of the stray? And if he finds it, amen, I say to you, he rejoices more over it than over the ninety-nine that did not stray. In just the same way, it is not the will of your heavenly Father that one of these little ones be lost."

God's Word strikes the heart. What word or phrase touched your heart?

_____

_____

What does it reveal about God's love and mercy that He is willing to leave the ninety-nine in search of one sheep?

_____

_____

Ask this question in prayer: "Jesus, Good Shepherd, You taught the disciples about the Father's love by this teaching. How can I search for the lost sheep in my daily life?" Write down what He says to you.

_____

_____

_____

"My sheep hear my voice; I know them, and they follow me."
— John 10:27

— Preparing the Manger of Your Heart —

Spend time praying for those people who do not know of God's merciful love. Pray for the lost sheep.

Matthew 11:28–30

Jesus said to the crowds: "Come to me, all you who labor and are burdened, and I will give you rest. Take my yoke upon you and learn from me, for I am meek and humble of heart; and you will find rest for yourselves. For my yoke is easy, and my burden light."

God's Word strikes the heart. What word or phrase touched your heart?

_____

_____

Jesus says, "I am meek and humble of heart." Read the meaning of meekness and humility on page 95. How does this knowledge help you to understand Jesus' love for you?

_____

_____

_____

How does it make you willing to give Him the burdens of your heart?

_____

_____

_____

It can be difficult to surrender our burdens, but Jesus wants us to rest in Him. Ask Him to teach you how to surrender everything to Him and trust. Write down He says to you.

_____

_____

_____

_____

— Preparing the Manger of Your Heart —

Sit quietly and reflect upon your life.
Surrender your sins and burdens to Him.

Matthew 11:11–15

Jesus said to the crowds: "Amen, I say to you, among those born of women there has been none greater than John the Baptist; yet the least in the kingdom of heaven is greater than he. From the days of John the Baptist until now, the kingdom of heaven suffers violence, and the violent are taking it by force. All the prophets and the law prophesied up to the time of John. And if you are willing to accept it, he is Elijah, the one who is to come. Whoever has ears ought to hear."

God's Word strikes the heart. What word or phrase touched your heart?

_____

_____

What does Jesus say about John the Baptist?

_____

_____

Jesus, Messiah, Your words were difficult for some people to accept. Often I hear Your Word proclaimed, but I fail to listen and act. In what ways can I be a better listener and therefore a more faithful disciple? (Write down what He says to you.)

_____

_____

_____

— Preparing the Manger of Your Heart —

Disconnect from a device to hear God's Word.

 **My Meditation**

2nd Friday of Advent

Matthew 11:16–19

Jesus said to the crowds: "To what shall I compare this generation? It is like children who sit in marketplaces and call to one another, 'We played the flute for you, but you did not dance, we sang a dirge but you did not mourn.' For John came neither eating nor drinking, and they said, 'He is possessed by a demon.' The Son of Man came eating and drinking and they said, 'Look, he is a glutton and a drunkard, a friend of tax collectors and sinners.' But wisdom is vindicated by her works."

God's Word strikes the heart. What word or phrase touched your heart?

_____

_____

Acedia is a form of "spiritual sorrow" (spiritual sloth) caused by neglecting one's relationship with God. This is what Jesus seems to be preaching to the crowds about—an attitude of "not caring." How do you think acedia is present today?

_____

_____

_____

"Jesus, show to me the ways I neglect establishing a relationship with You." Write down what He says to you.

_____

_____

_____

— Preparing the Manger of Your Heart —

Magnanimity is seeking with confidence to do great things in God, literally "having a large soul."

Recite the Magnanimity Prayer.

Sacred Heart of Jesus,
You loved us even to the point of death. Give me
a big heart! Give me Your Heart! Help me to love
others with all my heart!

MAGNANIMITY

Seeking with confidence to do great things for God

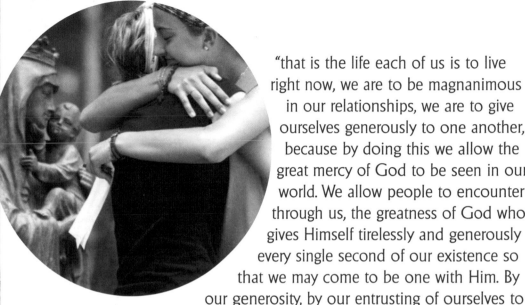

"that is the life each of us is to live right now, we are to be magnanimous in our relationships, we are to give ourselves generously to one another, because by doing this we allow the great mercy of God to be seen in our world. We allow people to encounter through us, the greatness of God who gives Himself tirelessly and generously every single second of our existence so that we may come to be one with Him. By our generosity, by our entrusting of ourselves to one another, by giving ourselves to one another, we open up a path for God within ourselves and within our world so that His mercy may come and visit upon all of us and His judgment may be lifted and we may experience the joys of eternal life." —excerpt taken from *The Genuine Class of Magnanimity*, Homily by Fr. Meyers, 3rd Sunday of Advent December 13, 2015

Your kindness should be known to all. The Lord is near.
—Philippians 4:5

GIVING OF MY VERY SELF   AN OPEN HEART

GENTLENESS   KINDNESS

2nd Saturday  of Advent

> ### Matthew 17:9A: 10–13
>
> As they were coming down from the mountain, the disciples asked Jesus, "Why do the scribes say that Elijah must come first?" He said in reply, "Elijah will indeed come and restore all things; but I tell you that Elijah has already come, and they did not recognize him but did to him whatever they pleased. So also will the Son of Man suffer at their hands." Then the disciples understood that he was speaking to them of John the Baptist.

God's Word strikes the heart. What word or phrase touched your heart?

_____

_____

Peter, James, and John had just seen the prophet Elijah on Mt. Tabor as Jesus was transfigured before them. [Elijah had courageously called people to repentance and was persecuted.] Jesus confirms the belief that Elijah was to come first and has already come. How is John the Baptist like Elijah?

_____

_____

_____

Ask this question in prayer: "Jesus, it is difficult to call people to conversion and repentance. How can I be like Elijah and John the Baptist by bearing witness to You?" Write down what He says to you.

_____

_____

_____

— Preparing the Manger of Your Heart —

Pray for Fortitude

Dear Jesus,
Alone I am weak, but with You I can do all things. Give
me the grace to be strong against temptations and
bold in proclaiming You and Your Church on earth.

HOLY FATHER'S HOMILY FOR THE THIRD SUNDAY OF ADVENT
POPE JOHN PAUL II

"Gaudete in Domino semper. Iterum dico: Gaudete! ... Dominus prope". "Rejoice in the Lord always, again I will say, Rejoice... The Lord is at hand" (Phil 4:4-5). It is from these words taken from St. Paul's letter to the Philippians, that this Sunday takes the liturgical name "Gaudete". Today the liturgy urges us to rejoice because the birth of the Lord is approaching: in fact it is only 10 days away.

In his Letter to the Thessalonians, the Apostle exhorts us thus: "Rejoice always, pray constantly, give thanks in all circumstances... May the God of peace himself sanctify you wholly; and may your spirit and soul and body be kept sound and blameless at the coming of our Lord Jesus Christ" (1 Thes 5:16–18; 23).

This is a typical *Advent exhortation.* Advent is the liturgical season that prepares us for the Lord's birth, but it is also the time of expectation for the *definitive return of Christ* for the last judgment, and St. Paul refers, in the first place, to this second coming. The very fact that the conclusion of the liturgical year coincides with the beginning of Advent suggests that "the beginning of the time of salvation is in some way linked to the "end of time". This exhortation typical of Advent always applies: "The Lord is at hand!".

In today's liturgy the prospect of Christ's coming at Christmas, so near now, seems to prevail. The echo of joy at the Messiah's birth resounds in the *Magnificat,* the canticle that wells up in Mary during her visit to the elderly wife of Zechariah. Elizabeth greets Mary with the words: "And why is this granted me, that the mother of my Lord should come to me? For behold, when the voice of your greeting came to my ears, the babe in my womb leaped for joy. And blessed is she who believed that there would be a fulfillment of what was spoken to her from the Lord" (Lk 1:43–45). Advanced in age and by now beyond all hope of possible motherhood, Elizabeth had realized that the extraordinary grace granted her was closely linked to the divine plan of salvation. The son who was to be born of her had been foreseen by God as the Precursor called to prepare the way for Christ (cf. Lk 1:76) And Mary replies with the words of the *Magnificat,* repeated in the responsorial psalm today: "My soul magnifies the Lord, and my spirit rejoices in God my Saviour, for he has regarded the low estate of his handmaiden… He who is mighty has done great things for me, and holy is his name" (Lk 1:46–49).

John the Baptist is one of the most significant biblical figures we meet during this important season of the liturgical year. In the fourth Gospel we read: "There was a man sent from God whose name was John. He came for testimony, to bear witness to the light that all might believe through him. He was not the light, but came to bear witness to the light" (Jn 1:6–8). To the question "Who are you?", John the Baptist responds: "I am not the Christ", nor Elijah, nor any other of the prophets (cf. Jn 1:19–20). And faced with the insistence of those sent from Jerusalem, he says: "I am the voice of one crying in the wilderness, 'Make straight the way of the Lord'" (Jn 1:23).

With this quote from Isaiah, in a certain sense he reveals his identity and clarifies his special role in the history of salvation. And when the representatives of the Sanhedrin ask him why he is baptizing, although he is neither the Messiah, nor Elijah, nor any other prophet, he answers: "I baptize with water; but among you stands one whom you do not know, even he who comes after me, the thong of whose sandal I am not worthy to untie" (Jn 1:26–27).

John the Baptist's witness re-echoes in the Advent verse: "The Lord is at hand!". The different perspectives of the night of Bethlehem and the baptism in the Jordan converge in the same truth: we must shake off our inertia and prepare the way of the Lord who comes.

The Lord Jesus is at hand at every moment of our life. He is at hand if we consider him in the perspective of Christmas, but he is also at hand if we look at him on the banks of the Jordan when he officially receives his messianic mission from the Father; lastly, he is at hand in the perspective of his return at the end of time.

Christ is at hand! He comes by virtue of the Holy Spirit to announce the Good News; he comes to cure and to set free to proclaim a time of grace and salvation, in order to begin, already on the night of Bethlehem, the work of the world's redemption.

Let us therefore rejoice and exult! The Lord is at hand; he is coming to save us. Amen!

Matthew 21:23–27

When Jesus had come into the temple area, the chief priests and the elders of the people approached him as he was teaching and said, "By what authority are you doing these things? And who gave you this authority?" Jesus said to them in reply, "I shall ask you one question, and if you answer it for me, then I shall tell you by what authority I do these things. Where was John's baptism from? Was it of heavenly or of human origin?" They discussed this among themselves and said, "If we say 'Of heavenly origin,' he will say to us, 'Then why did you not believe him?' But if we say, 'Of human origin,' we fear the crowd, for they all regard John as a prophet." So they said to Jesus in reply, "We do not know." He himself said to them, "Neither shall I tell you by what authority I do these things."

God's Word strikes the heart. What word or phrase touched your heart?

_____

_____

The chief priests and elders were unable to answer Jesus' question and responded, "We do not know." Why do you think they responded that way? Do you think they were they afraid or embarrassed?

_____

_____

_____

"Jesus, I sincerely desire to be taught by You. Show me what I hesitate to talk to You about through embarrassment or fear." Write down what He says to you.

_____

_____

_____

DOCILITY

Willingness to be taught

"But I must receive the Spirit that leads me to the Word with docility, and this docility, not to resist the Spirit, will lead me to this way of life, in this way of acting. To receive the Word with discretion, to know the Word, and to ask the Spirit for grace to make it known, and then to give space for this seed to sprout and grow in those attitudes of goodness, mildness, benevolence, peace, charity, mastery of self: all that does The Christian style." —Pope Francis

"Speak, for your servant is listening."
—Samuel 3:10

TEACHABLE   CHILDLIKE

HUMBLE   WILLING SPIRIT

Matthew 21:28–32

Jesus said to the chief priests and the elders of the people: "What is your opinion? A man had two sons. He came to the first and said, 'Son, go out and work in the vineyard today.' The son said in reply, 'I will not,' but afterwards he changed his mind and went. The man came to the other son and gave the same order. He said in reply, 'Yes, sir,' but did not go. Which of the two did his father's will?" They answered, "The first." Jesus said to them, "Amen, I say to you, tax collectors and prostitutes are entering the Kingdom of God before you. When John came to you in the way of righteousness, you did not believe him; but tax collectors and prostitutes did. Yet even when you saw that, you did not later change your minds and believe."

God's Word strikes the heart. What word or phrase touched your heart?

_____

_____

_____

The first son refused to do what his father told him to do. How did the first son respond? Why, then, does Jesus praise him as the one who "did his father's will?"

_____

_____

_____

Ask this question in prayer: "Jesus, show me an area in my life where my words do not match my actions. What virtue do I need to cultivate in order to overcome this?" Write down what He says to you.

_____

_____

_____

— Preparing the Manger of Your Heart —

Recite the Act of Faith prayer.

O my God, I firmly believe that You are one God in three divine Persons, Father, Son, and Holy Spirit. I believe that Your divine Son became man and died for our sins, and that He will come to judge the living and the dead. I believe these and all the truths which the holy Catholic Church teaches, because in revealing them You can neither deceive nor be deceived.

✳ **My Meditation**

Luke 7:18B–23

At that time, John summoned two of his disciples and sent them to the Lord to ask, "Are you the one who is to come, or should we look for another?" When the men came to the Lord, they said, "John the Baptist has sent us to you to ask, 'Are you the one who is to come, or should we look for another?'" At that time Jesus cured many of their diseases, sufferings, and evil spirits; he also granted sight to many who were blind. And Jesus said to them in reply, "Go and tell John what you have seen and heard: the blind regain their sight, the lame walk, lepers are cleansed, the deaf hear, the dead are raised, the poor have the good news proclaimed to them. And blessed is the one who takes no offense at me."

God's Word strikes the heart. What word or phrase touched your heart?

_____

_____

John the Baptist sent two of his disciples to ask Jesus, "Are you the one who is to come, or should we look for another?" (Luke 7:19) How did Jesus answer their question?

_____

_____

_____

Why do you think John the Baptist didn't go to see Jesus? Do you think he believed and knew in his heart?

_____

_____

_____

— Preparing the Manger of Your Heart —

Spend time in prayer expressing your gratitude for all the
infirmities (sins) of your soul that God has healed.

Luke 7:24–30

When the messengers of John had left, Jesus began to speak to the crowds about John. "What did you go out to the desert to see—a reed swayed by the wind? Then what did you go out to see? Someone dressed in fine garments? Those who dress luxuriously and live sumptuously are found in royal palaces. Then what did you go out to see? A prophet? Yes, I tell you, and more than a prophet. This is the one about whom scripture says: 'Behold, I am sending my messenger ahead of you, he will prepare your way before you.' I tell you, among those born of women, no one is greater than John; yet the least in the kingdom of God is greater than he." (All the people who listened, including the tax collectors, and who were baptized with the baptism of John, acknowledged the righteousness of God; but the Pharisees and scholars of the law, who were not baptized by him, rejected the plan of God for themselves.)

God's Word strikes the heart. What word or phrase touched your heart?

_____

_____

Jesus said that John was "more than a prophet." In fact, he was a messenger. Identify one example of John being a messenger announcing the presence of Jesus by word or action.

_____

_____

_____

How did the Pharisees and scholars respond to the messengers? Why did they respond this way?

_____

_____

_____

"Jesus, Messiah, John fearlessly preached about Your coming and encouraged people to listen to You. Show me How I can listen to Your voice." Write down what you heard Him say to you.

_____

_____

_____

_____

— Preparing the Manger of Your Heart —

Write down ways you can be a "messenger" to others.

_____

_____

_____

_____

_____

_____

John 5:33–36

You sent emissaries to John, and he testified to the truth. I do not accept testimony from a human being, but I say this so that you may be saved. He was a burning and shining lamp,* and for a while you were content to rejoice in his light. But I have testimony greater than John's. The works that the Father gave me to accomplish, these works that I perform testify on my behalf that the Father has sent me.

God's Word strikes the heart. What word or phrase touched your heart?

_____

_____

Who has God placed in your life as a "burning and shining lamp" so that you could be saved? How did they do this?

_____

_____

_____

If someone looked at your life, would your works testify to Jesus? How?

_____

_____

_____

"Jesus, make known to me the works the Father gives me to accomplish today."
Write down what He says to you.

_____

_____

_____

_____

— Preparing the Manger of Your Heart —

Write a prayer thanking God for the witness of others
that have led you to know Him.

_____

_____

_____

_____

AT LAST HIS MIGHTY VOICE IS HEARD

The star illuminates the cave in Bethlehem,
while the angels song of "Gloria"
serenades the shepherds
tending their sheep.

Three magi journey from afar.
In awe, wonder, and bended knee,
they adore the Child with His mother
offering gold, frankincense, and myrrh.

Frozen with greed and desire for power,
Herod surreptitiously searches for the King
Who threatens his supremacy.

Hidden, in the crevice of the cave,
a still, small noise is heard.
The cry of the Christ-child pierces the darkness
—God has spoken—
Man has heard the voice of God.

Consoled in the warm embrace of His mother,
She will nurse, nurture, and adore Him.
—Love receiving love—

He "enters" in pure flesh,
tears streaming down His precious face.
He "leaves" in torn flesh,
blood streaming down His precious face.
Incarnation and Redemption converge
in His gift of vulnerability.
—Love poured forth—

At last His mighty voice is heard.

Matthew 1:1–17

The book of the genealogy of Jesus Christ, the son of David, the son of Abraham.

Abraham became the father of Isaac, Isaac the father of Jacob, Jacob the father of Judah and his brothers. Judah became the father of Perez and Zerah, whose mother was Tamar. Perez became the father of Hezron, Hezron the father of Ram, Ram the father of Amminadab. Amminadab became the father of Nahshon, Nahshon the father of Salmon, Salmon the father of Boaz, whose mother was Rahab. Boaz became the father of Obed, whose mother was Ruth. Obed became the father of Jesse, Jesse the father of David the king.

David became the father of Solomon, whose mother had been the wife of Uriah. Solomon became the father of Rehoboam, Rehoboam the father of Abijah, Abijah the father of Asaph. Asaph became the father of Jehoshaphat, Jehoshaphat the father of Joram, Joram the father of Uzziah. Uzziah became the father of Jotham, Jotham the father of Ahaz, Ahaz the father of Hezekiah. Hezekiah became the father of Manasseh, Manasseh the father of Amos, Amos the father of Josiah. Josiah became the father of Jechoniah and his brothers at the time of the Babylonian exile.

After the Babylonian exile, Jechoniah became the father of Shealtiel, Shealtiel the father of Zerubbabel, Zerubbabel the father of Abiud. Abiud became the father of Eliakim, Eliakim the father of Azor, Azor the father of Zadok. Zadok became the father of Achim, Achim the father of Eliud, Eliud the father of Eleazar. Eleazar became the father of Matthan, Matthan the father of Jacob, Jacob the father of Joseph, the husband of Mary. Of her was born Jesus who is called the Christ.

Thus the total number of generations from Abraham to David is fourteen generations; from David to the Babylonian exile, fourteen generations; from the Babylonian exile to the Christ, fourteen generations.

The word Advent means "coming," and reading Jesus' genealogy enables us to enter into the Israelites' longing for the Messiah. How can this spirit of anticipation help you prepare for the birth of Jesus?

Think about your own genealogy (ancestors). How are they different? Except Mary, the people listed were sinners. Why is this important?

_____

_____

_____

Ask this question in prayer: "Jesus, Savior, You came to save sinners. How can I trust in Your mercy if there are people in my family who have hurt me?" Write down what He says to you.

_____

_____

_____

— Preparing the Manger of Your Heart —

**Pray for people who suffer because of a sad
and broken family.**

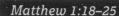

This is how the birth of Jesus Christ came about.

When his mother Mary was betrothed to Joseph, but before they lived together, she was found with child through the Holy Spirit. Joseph her husband, since he was a righteous man, yet unwilling to expose her to shame, decided to divorce her quietly. Such was his intention when, behold, the angel of the Lord appeared to him in a dream and said, "Joseph, son of David, do not be afraid to take Mary your wife into your home. For it is through the Holy Spirit that this child has been conceived in her. She will bear a son and you are to name him Jesus, because he will save his people from their sins." All this took place to fulfill what the Lord had said through the prophet:

Behold, the virgin shall be with child and bear a son,
and they shall name him Emmanuel,

which means "God is with us." When Joseph awoke, he did as the angel of the Lord had commanded him and took his wife into his home. He had no relations with her until she bore a son, and he named him Jesus.

God's Word strikes the heart. What word or phrase touched your heart?

_____

_____

Joseph had decided to divorce Mary quietly. What does this reveal about Joseph's character?

_____

_____

_____

An angel appeared to Joseph in a dream. What was his response to the message? How was Joseph's response different from Zechariah's?

_____

_____

_____

"Emmanuel" means God is with us. "Jesus, what do You want me to learn by Joseph's trust in the angel's message and Your name meaning 'God is with us'?" Write down what He says to you.

_____

_____

_____

— Preparing the Manger of Your Heart —

Spend time reflecting upon the ways that "God is with us." How does this truth increase your faith and hope in God's loving plan for your life?

Luke 1:5–25

In the days of Herod, King of Judea, there was a priest named Zechariah of the priestly division of Abijah; his wife was from the daughters of Aaron, and her name was Elizabeth. Both were righteous in the eyes of God, observing all the commandments and ordinances of the Lord blamelessly. But they had no child, because Elizabeth was barren and both were advanced in years.

Once when he was serving as priest in his division's turn before God, according to the practice of the priestly service, he was chosen by lot to enter the sanctuary of the Lord to burn incense. Then, when the whole assembly of the people was praying outside at the hour of the incense offering, the angel of the Lord appeared to him, standing at the right of the altar of incense. Zechariah was troubled by what he saw, and fear came upon him.

But the angel said to him, "Do not be afraid, Zechariah, because your prayer has been heard. Your wife Elizabeth will bear you a son, and you shall name him John. And you will have joy and gladness, and many will rejoice at his birth, for he will be great in the sight of the Lord. He will drink neither wine nor strong drink. He will be filled with the Holy Spirit even from his mother's womb, and he will turn many of the children of Israel to the Lord their God. He will go before him in the spirit and power of Elijah to turn the hearts of fathers toward children and the disobedient to the understanding of the righteous, to prepare a people fit for the Lord."

Then Zechariah said to the angel, "How shall I know this? For I am an old man, and my wife is advanced in years." And the angel said to him in reply, "I am Gabriel, who stand before God. I was sent to speak to you and to announce to you this good news. But now you will be speechless and unable to talk until the day these things take place, because you did not believe my words, which will be fulfilled at their proper time." Meanwhile the people were waiting for Zechariah and were amazed that he stayed so long in the sanctuary. But when he came out, he was unable to speak to them, and they realized that he had seen a vision in the sanctuary. He was gesturing to them but remained mute.

Then, when his days of ministry were completed, he went home. After this time his wife Elizabeth conceived, and she went into seclusion for five months, saying, "So has the Lord done for me at a time when he has seen fit to take away my disgrace before others."

God's Word strikes the heart. What word or phrase touched your heart?

_____

_____

The angel Gabriel joyfully communicates to Zechariah that his prayer has been heard. Write down what Gabriel says about John. (For example: "He will be great in the sight of the Lord.")

_____

_____

_____

Even though Zechariah heard the angel's message, he struggled to fully accept it. For a period of time, he was speechless (mute). How can silence help us to understand difficult things?

_____

_____

Zechariah had trouble believing the message announced by the angel, possibly because it seemed too good to be true. Ask Jesus this question in prayer: "Jesus, what good things do You especially want me to believe about You?" Write down what you hear Him say.

_____

_____

_____

_____

— Preparing the Manger of Your Heart —

Spend time in silence before the Lord and ask Jesus to help you surrender your doubt or lack of faith to Him.

Luke 1:26–38

The angel Gabriel was sent from God to a town of Galilee called Nazareth, to a virgin betrothed to a man named Joseph, of the house of David, and the virgin's name was Mary. And coming to her, he said, "Hail, full of grace! The Lord is with you." But she was greatly troubled at what was said and pondered what sort of greeting this might be. Then the angel said to her, "Do not be afraid, Mary, for you have found favor with God. Behold, you will conceive in your womb and bear a son, and you shall name him Jesus. He will be great and will be called Son of the Most High, and the Lord God will give him the throne of David his father, and he will rule over the house of Jacob forever, and of his Kingdom there will be no end." But Mary said to the angel, "How can this be, since I have no relations with a man?" And the angel said to her in reply, "The Holy Spirit will come upon you, and the power of the Most High will overshadow you. Therefore the child to be born will be called holy, the Son of God. And behold, Elizabeth, your relative, has also conceived a son in her old age, and this is the sixth month for her who was called barren; for nothing will be impossible for God." Mary said, "Behold, I am the handmaid of the Lord. May it be done to me according to your word." Then the angel departed from her.

God's Word strikes the heart. What word or phrase touched your heart?

_____

_____

Write down Mary's response to the angel Gabriel.

_____

_____

_____

To obey means "to hear." Describe how the virtues of docility and humility enabled Mary to obey God (see pages 6 and 7).

_____

_____

_____

Ask Jesus this question in prayer. "Jesus, Your mother prayerfully pondered Gabriel's message. How can I be more patient and ponder God's will for my life?" Write down what He says to you.

_____

_____

_____

Mary said, "Behold, I am the handmaid of the Lord. May it be done to me according to your word." Then the angel departed from her. —Luke 1:38

— Preparing the Manger of Your Heart —

Say "yes" when someone asks you to help them.

Luke 1:39–45

Mary set out and traveled to the hill country in haste to a town of Judah, where she entered the house of Zechariah and greeted Elizabeth. When Elizabeth heard Mary's greeting, the infant leaped in her womb, and Elizabeth, filled with the Holy Spirit, cried out in a loud voice and said, "Blessed are you among women, and blessed is the fruit of your womb. And how does this happen to me, that the mother of my Lord should come to me? For at the moment the sound of your greeting reached my ears, the infant in my womb leaped for joy. Blessed are you who believed that what was spoken to you by the Lord would be fulfilled."

God's Word strikes the heart. What word or phrase touched your heart?

_____

_____

What virtue made Mary go in haste to her cousin, Elizabeth? How can you live out this virtue today?

_____

_____

_____

Joy is a fruit of Charity. What makes you joyful?

_____

_____

_____

You, too, are called to be a source of joy to others. Ask Jesus in prayer to show you how you can be like Mary. Write down what He says to you.

_____

_____

_____

_____

... *"there is more happiness*
in giving, than in receiving."
—Acts 20:35

— Preparing the Manger of Your Heart —

Mary went in haste to visit her cousin, Elizabeth.
Today, give of yourself to someone in need.

Luke 1:46–56

"My soul proclaims the greatness of the Lord; my spirit rejoices in God my savior, for he has looked upon his lowly servant. From this day all generations will call me blessed: the Almighty has done great things for me, and holy is his Name. He has mercy on those who fear him in every generation. He has shown the strength of his arm, and has scattered the proud in their conceit. He has cast down the mighty from their thrones and has lifted up the lowly. He has filled the hungry with good things, and the rich he has sent away empty. He has come to the help of his servant Israel for he remembered his promise of mercy, the promise he made to our fathers, to Abraham and his children for ever."

Mary remained with Elizabeth about three months and then returned to her home.

God's Word strikes the heart. What word or phrase touched your heart?

_____

_____

Mary praised God for fulfilling His promise of salvation. How is Mary a model of the virtue of humility?

_____

_____

_____

Jesus, Son of Mary, show me how the Father's plan has been fulfilled in my own life. Teach me how to praise Him as Your mother did. Spirit of Truth, let me see God. Help me to write my prayer of praise.

_____

_____

_____

"My spirit rejoices in God my savior. For he has looked upon his handmaid's lowliness; behold, from now on will all ages call me blessed. The Mighty One has done great things for me, and holy is his name." —Luke 1:47–48

— Preparing the Manger of Your Heart —

Spend ten minutes in prayer asking Mary to
show you how to be more like her.
Listen carefully to her gentle voice.

Luke 1:57–66

When the time arrived for Elizabeth to have her child she gave birth to a son. Her neighbors and relatives heard that the Lord had shown his great mercy toward her, and they rejoiced with her. When they came on the eighth day to circumcise the child, they were going to call him Zechariah after his father, but his mother said in reply, "No. He will be called John." But they answered her, "There is no one among your relatives who has this name." So they made signs, asking his father what he wished him to be called. He asked for a tablet and wrote, "John is his name," and all were amazed. Immediately his mouth was opened, his tongue freed, and he spoke blessing God. Then fear came upon all their neighbors, and all these matters were discussed throughout the hill country of Judea. All who heard these things took them to heart, saying, "What, then, will this child be? For surely the hand of the Lord was with him."

God's Word strikes the heart. What word or phrase touched your heart?

_____

_____

When we are silent, we are better able to listen and see things more clearly. Describe how silence prepared Zechariah to accept God's will.

_____

_____

_____

Zechariah had spent months in silence. After he wrote the name of his son, he could speak. What is significant about his first words?

_____

_____

_____

Ask this question in prayer: "Jesus, as I listen to you in the silence of my heart, what do you desire to say?" Write down what He says to you.

_____

_____

_____

_____

— Preparing the Manger of Your Heart —

Unplug all devices today and spend time in silence.
Prepare the manger of your heart for the coming of
the Infant Jesus.

Luke 1:67–79

Zechariah his father, filled with the Holy Spirit, prophesied, saying:

"Blessed be the Lord, the God of Israel; for he has come to his people and set them free. He has raised up for us a mighty Savior, born of the house of his servant David. Through his prophets he promised of old that he would save us from our enemies, from the hands of all who hate us. He promised to show mercy to our fathers and to remember his holy covenant. This was the oath he swore to our father Abraham: to set us free from the hand of our enemies, free to worship him without fear, holy and righteous in his sight all the days of our life. You, my child, shall be called the prophet of the Most High, for you will go before the Lord to prepare his way, to give his people knowledge of salvation by the forgiveness of their sins. In the tender compassion of our God the dawn from on high shall break upon us, to shine on those who dwell in darkness and the shadow of death, and to guide our feet into the way of peace."

God's Word strikes the heart. What word or phrase touched your heart?

_____

_____

How does Zechariah's canticle of praise show that he believes in God's promise of salvation?

_____

_____

_____

Write a prayer of praise and thanksgiving for all God has given you.

_____

_____

_____

_____

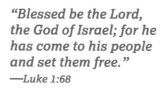

"Blessed be the Lord, the God of Israel; for he has come to his people and set them free."
—*Luke 1:68*

— Preparing the Manger of Your Heart —

Spend time with the Lord praising Him for
sending His only begotten Son.

Luke 2:1–14

In those days a decree went out from Caesar Augustus that the whole world should be enrolled. This was the first enrollment, when Quirinius was governor of Syria. So all went to be enrolled, each to his own town. And Joseph too went up from Galilee from the town of Nazareth to Judea, to the city of David that is called Bethlehem, because he was of the house and family of David, to be enrolled with Mary, his betrothed, who was with child. While they were there, the time came for her to have her child, and she gave birth to her firstborn son. She wrapped him in swaddling clothes and laid him in a manger, because there was no room for them in the inn.

Now there were shepherds in that region living in the fields and keeping the night watch over their flock. The angel of the Lord appeared to them and the glory of the Lord shone around them, and they were struck with great fear. The angel said to them, "Do not be afraid; for behold, I proclaim to you good news of great joy that will be for all the people. For today in the city of David a savior has been born for you who is Christ and Lord. And this will be a sign for you: you will find an infant wrapped in swaddling clothes and lying in a manger." And suddenly there was a multitude of the heavenly host with the angel, praising God and saying:

"Glory to God in the highest
and on earth peace to those on whom his favor rests."

To surrender to God's will requires an act of faith. Mary said "yes," and the "Word became fiesh."

YEAR A

YEAR: 2019, 2022, 2025

Week 1: *Matthew 24:37-44*

Week 2: *Matthew 3:1–12*

Week 3: *Matthew 11:2–11*

Week 4: *Matthew 1:18–24*

YEAR B

YEAR: 2020, 2023, 2026

Week 1: *Mark 13:33–37*

Week 2: *Mark 1:1–8*

Week 3: *John 1:6–8; 19–28*

Week 4: *Luke 1:26–38*

YEAR C

YEAR: 2018, 2021, 2024

Week 1: *Luke 21:25–28, 34–36*

Week 2: *Luke 3:1–6*

Week 3: *Luke 3:10–18*

Week 4: *Luke 1:39–45*

December 8

Genesis 3:9–15; 20

After the man, Adam, had eaten of the tree, the LORD God called to the man and asked him, "Where are you?" He answered, "I heard you in the garden; but I was afraid, because I was naked, so I hid myself." Then he asked, "Who told you that you were naked? You have eaten, then, from the tree of which I had forbidden you to eat!" The man replied, "The woman whom you put here with me she gave me fruit from the tree, and so I ate it." The LORD God then asked the woman, "Why did you do such a thing?" The woman answered, "The serpent tricked me into it, so I ate it."

Then the LORD God said to the serpent: "Because you have done this, you shall be banned from all the animals and from all the wild creatures; on your belly shall you crawl, and dirt shall you eat all the days of your life. I will put enmity between you and the woman, and between your offspring and hers; he will strike at your head, while you strike at his heel."

The man called his wife Eve, because she became the mother of all the living.

God's Word strikes the heart. What word or phrase touched your heart?

_____

_____

What did Adam and Eve do after they sinned? Why?

_____

_____

After Adam and Eve disobeyed God's command, they tried to hide from God. Yet God called out to Adam, "Where are you?" What does this reveal about God's love toward us?

_____

_____

How did Adam and Eve respond to God's question?

_____

_____

What did God say to the serpent?

_____

_____

_____

Who is the woman referred to by God? What will she do?

_____

_____

Ask this question in prayer: "Father, most merciful and just, Adam and Eve suffered the consequence of their disobedience, but You also searched for them in the garden. Show me how I try to hide my sins from You." Write down what He says to you.

_____

_____

_____

Genesis 3:15 states: "I will put enmity between you and the woman, and between your offspring and hers; he will strike at your head, while you strike at his heel." This is known as the Protoevangelium ("first gospel"): the first announcement of the Messiah and Redeemer, of a battle between the serpent and the Woman, and of the final victory of a descendant of hers. —CCC, 410

December 12

From a report by Don Antonio Valeriano, a Native American author of the sixteenth century
The Voice of the Turtledove Has Been Heard in Our Land

At daybreak one Saturday morning in 1531, on the very first days of the month of December, an Indian named Juan Diego was going from the village where he lived to Tlatelolco in order to take part in divine worship and listen to God's commandments. When he came near the hill called Tepeyac, dawn had already come, and Juan Diego heard someone calling him from the very top of the hill: "Juanito, Juan Dieguito."

He went up the hill and caught sight of a lady of unearthly grandeur whose clothing was as radiant as the sun. She said to him in words both gentle and courteous: "Juanito, the humblest of my children, know and understand that I am the ever virgin Mary, Mother of the true God through whom all things live. It is my ardent desire that a church be erected here so that in it I can show and bestow my love, compassion, help, and protection to all who inhabit this land and to those others who love me, that they might call upon and confide in me. Go to the Bishop of Mexico to make known to him what I greatly desire. Go and put all your efforts into this."

When Juan Diego arrived in the presence of the Bishop, Fray Juan de Zumarraga, a Franciscan, the latter did not seem to believe Juan Diego and answered: "Come another time, and I will listen at leisure."

Juan Diego returned to the hilltop where the Heavenly Lady was waiting, and he said to her: "My Lady, my maiden, I presented your message to the Bishop, but it seemed that he did not think it was the truth. For this reason I beg you to entrust your message to someone more illustrious who might convey it in order that they may believe it, for I am only an insignificant man."

She answered him: "Humblest of my sons, I ask that tomorrow you again go to see the Bishop and tell him that I, the ever virgin holy Mary, Mother of God, am the one who personally sent you."

But on the following day, Sunday, the Bishop again did not believe Juan Diego and told him that some sign was necessary so that he could believe that it was the Heavenly Lady herself who sent him. And then he dismissed Juan Diego.

On Monday Juan Diego did not return. His uncle, Juan Bernardino, became very ill, and at night asked Juan to go to Tlatelolco at daybreak to call a priest to hear his confession.

Juan Diego set out on Tuesday, but he went around the hill and passed on the other side, toward the east, so as to arrive quickly in Mexico City and to avoid being detained by the Heavenly Lady. But she came out to meet him on that side of the hill and said to him: "Listen

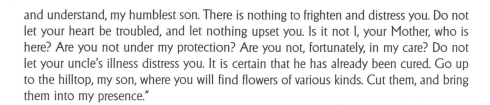

and understand, my humblest son. There is nothing to frighten and distress you. Do not let your heart be troubled, and let nothing upset you. Is it not I, your Mother, who is here? Are you not under my protection? Are you not, fortunately, in my care? Do not let your uncle's illness distress you. It is certain that he has already been cured. Go up to the hilltop, my son, where you will find flowers of various kinds. Cut them, and bring them into my presence."

When Juan Diego reached the peak, he was astonished that so many Castilian roses had burst forth at a time when the frost was severe. He carried the roses in the folds of his tilma (mantle) to the Heavenly Lady. She said to him: "My son, this is the proof and the sign which you will bring to the Bishop so that he will see my will in it. You are my ambassador, very worthy of trust."

Juan Diego set out on his way, now content and sure of succeeding. On arriving in the Bishop's presence, he told him: "My lord, I did what you asked. The Heavenly Lady complied with your request and fulfilled it. She sent me to the hilltop to cut some Castilian roses and told me to bring them to you in person. And this I am doing, so that you can see in them the sign you seek in order to carry out her will. Here they are; receive them."

He immediately opened up his white mantle, and as all the different Castilian roses scattered to the ground, there was drawn on the cloak and suddenly appeared the precious image of the ever virgin Mary, Mother of God, in the same manner as it is today and is kept in her shrine of Tepeyac.

The whole city was stirred and came to see and admire her venerable image and to offer prayers to her; and following the command which the same Heavenly Lady gave to Juan Bernardino when she restored him to health, they called her by the name that she herself had used: "the ever virgin holy Mary of Guadalupe."

"Listen and let it penetrate your heart…do not be troubled or weighed down with grief. Do not fear any illness or vexation, anxiety or pain. Am I not here who am your Mother? Are you not under my shadow and protection? Am I not your fountain of life? Are you not in the folds of my mantle? In the crossing of my arms? Is there anything else you need?"

(Our Lady's words to her servant Juan Diego)

LIVING AS A

DISCIPLE OF CHRIST

HOLINESS DOES NOT CONSIST OF DOING EXTRAORDINARY THINGS. IT CONSISTS IN ACCEPTING, WITH A SMILE, WHATEVER JESUS SENDS US. IT CONSISTS IN ACCEPTING AND FOLLOWING THE WILL OF GOD.
—ST. MOTHER TERESA OF CALCUTTA

My Life in Christ

"Remain in me, as I remain in you. Just as a branch cannot bear fruit on its own unless it remains on the vine, so neither can you unless you remain in me" (John 15:4).

The Dominican saint from the Tuscany region of Italy, Catherine of Siena, gave an analogy that echoes Christ's discourse on the vine and branches. "The soul is in God and God in the soul, just as the fish is in the sea and the sea is in the fish." Just as a fish takes in the sea to survive, so must a disciple remain grafted on the vine to live and bear fruit.

By allowing the Word of God to touch our hearts, we come to know the Person of Christ. Once our minds have grasped the truth of His Words, our hearts follow and we desire only to "remain in His love." The "vineyard" of our heart must be cultivated and tended by the vine grower, who is the Father. The pruning takes place through self-knowledge and identifying the branches deadened by sin and not grafted unto Christ the vine. This requires a personal commitment to free your heart from distractions sin and vice. Sin has deep roots and can strangle the sap of love needed to nourish the branches of virtue.

As you meditate on God's Word, let Him touch your heart and renew your commitment to be His disciple. The path to interior freedom and happiness is found by remaining in Him as a branch grafted on the vine, or in the words of St. Catherine, "The soul is in God and God in the soul, just as the fish is in the sea and the sea is in the fish."

✝ CONVERSION

The world offers you comfort. But you were not made for comfort, you were made for greatness.
—Pope Benedict XVI

pg.
78

 PRAYER

Christian prayer should go further: to the knowledge of the love of the Lord Jesus, to union with him. (CCC 2708)

pg.
86

✝ VIRTUE

Virtue is what one does passionately; Vice is what one cannot stop doing because of passion. —St. Augustine

pg. 92

❤ GIFT OF SELF

**The worst prison would be a closed heart.
—St. Pope John Paul II**

pg. 96

"I AM THE VINE, YOU ARE THE BRANCHES. HE WHO ABIDES IN ME, AND I IN HIM, HE IT IS THAT BEARS MUCH FRUIT, FOR APART FROM ME YOU CAN DO NOTHING. IF A MAN DOES NOT ABIDE IN ME, HE IS CAST FORTH AS A BRANCH AND WITHERS, AND THE BRANCHES ARE GATHERED, THROWN INTO THE FIRE AND BURNED."
— John 15: 5–6

At Baptism, every Christian is immersed into the water, symbolizing burial into Christ's death and rising in Him as a 'new creature' (*CCC*, §1214).

The virtues and gifts of the Holy Spirit are infused in the life of Christians and disposes them to live in relationship with the Holy Trinity.

By recognizing your sinfulness in light of the virtues and gifts of the Holy Spirit, you are able to receive God's merciful forgiveness. The 'ways of turning away from happiness' serve as a general guideline to assist with understanding how you can sin against a virtue or gift and impede God's grace from operating within your life.

Regular confession and a willingness to change patterns of sin opens your interior life to the love of Christ, which animates the growth of the virtues and gifts and enables you to be receptive to the promptings of the Spirit. By abiding in His grace and love, you are transformed from within and freed to live in happiness, striving for Eternal Beatitude.

The practice of all the virtues is animated and inspired by charity, which 'binds everything together in perfect harmony' (Colossians 3:14, *CCC*, §1827).

DAILY EXAMINATION

As a disciple of Christ, you are called to daily conversion. That is, striving each day to live in truth and freedom. A daily examination enables you to Experience God's mercy and start each day anew in Christ.

✝ **PRESENCE:** Place yourself in God's presence

✝ **PRAISE AND GRATITUDE:** Recall the blessings of the day – joys/sorrows

✝ **PROCESS:** Reflect upon the events of the day (your thoughts and feelings)

✝ **PENANCE AND CONVERSION:** Acknowledge your sins and resolve to change

✝ **PLAN AND PROMISE:** Intentionally plan for a new day to live receptive to God's grace

RITE OF THE SACRAMENT OF RECONCILIATION

- Greet the priest.
- Make the Sign of the Cross.
- Listen as the priest prays.
- Say, "Bless me, Father, for I have sinned. It has been (tell how long it has been) since my last confession."
- Tell your sins. You can speak about anything that is bothering you.
- Listen to the priest's advice.
- Accept your penance.
- Pray and act of contrition.
- Receive absolution, silently making the Sign of the Cross. Respond "Amen."
- Priest says "Give thanks to the Lord, for He is good."
- Response, "His mercy endures forever."
- Say, "Thank You, Father."
- Make sure you do your penance.

ACT OF CONTRITION

O my God, I am heartily sorry for having offended Thee and I detest all my sins because I dread the loss of heaven and the pains of hell. But most of all because they have offended Thee my God who art all good and deserving of all my love. I firmly resolve with the help of Thy grace to confess my sins, to do penance and to amend my life. Amen.

BELOW AND ON THE FOLLOWING PAGES, THE 'WAYS OF TURNING AWAY FROM HAPPINESS' SERVE AS A GENERAL GUIDELINE TO ASSIST WITH UNDERSTANDING HOW ONE CAN SIN AGAINST A VIRTUE OR GIFT AND IMPEDE GOD'S GRACE FROM OPERATING WITHIN ONE'S LIFE.

SEEING WITH FAITH

FAITH: ENABLES ONE TO KNOW GOD AND ALL THAT HE HAS REVEALED

GIFT OF UNDERSTANDING: Enables one to see more deeply into the mysteries of the faith and to judge with certainty all created things

GIFT OF KNOWLEDGE: Guides one in knowing what to believe and how to share it with others

WAYS OF TURNING AWAY FROM HAPPINESS

UNBELIEF OR INFIDELITY: Have I refused to accept the truths of the faith? Have I been selective in my acceptance of Church teachings?

HERESY: Have I led others astray by teaching/condoning/promoting things contrary to Church teaching?

APOSTASY: Have I become a public scandal to my Catholic faith through bad example or public denunciation of our Church's truths?

BLASPHEMY: Have I held God in contempt through my speech (swearing), actions or thoughts? Have I held priests, religious or anything that is sacred in contempt (i.e. the rosary, scapular, the Sacraments)?

BLINDNESS OF MIND (ARISES FROM LUST): Have I neglected my prayer/spiritual life? Are fulfilling my passions more important than attending to my spiritual life?

DULLNESS OF SENSE (ARISES FROM GLUTTONY): Have I become lazy in seeking the truths of the faith? Have I become complacent in accepting what the Church teaches?

ABIDING WITH HOPE

HOPE: Enables one to desire God above all things and to trust Him for personal salvation

GIFT OF FEAR OF THE LORD: Brings forth the fear of offending God by sin

HUMILITY: Awareness that all one's gifts come from God and the appreciation for the gifts of others

WAYS OF TURNING AWAY FROM HAPPINESS

DESPAIR: Have I thought that God could not forgive me my sins? Has my spiritual laziness (acedia) or unchastity caused me to lose hope in God's mercy?

PRESUMPTION: Have I committed sin by presuming God's forgiveness? Have I relied solely on my own capabilities as sufficient to handle anything?

ACEDIA: Have I neglected to observe the Lord's day? Am I unable to pursue and maintain a relationship with God? Do work and other activities consume my interests?

BURNING WITH CHARITY

CHARITY: Enables one to love as God Himself loves; includes loving God above all things and one's neighbor as oneself

GIFT OF WISDOM: Moves one to order one's life according to God's will

KINDNESS: Expressing genuine concern about the well-being of others, anticipating the needs of others

GENEROSITY: Giving of oneself in a willing, cheerful manner for the good of others

WAYS OF TURNING AWAY FROM HAPPINESS

HATRED OF GOD: Have I hated God as a result of my own pride and envy? Have I hated God because of my distaste/disdain for the penalty of sin? Have I hated God for some evil that has befallen me?

ENVY: Have I rejoiced in someone else's misfortune? Have I been jealous of others?

DISCORD/CONTENTION: Do I vehemently argue a point even when I know I might be wrong?

FOLLY: Have I made poor decisions in regards to the good of my soul because I am too attached to material things?

 **LOVING** **WITH JUSTICE**

JUSTICE: ENABLES ONE TO GIVE TO EACH , BEGINNING WITH GOD, WHAT IS DUE HIM

GIFT OF PIETY: Inclines one as a child of God to have devotion and honor to God as Father

GRATITUDE: Thankful disposition of mind and heart

OBEDIENCE: Assenting to rightful authority without hesitation or resistance

COURTESY: Treating other people with respect, recognizing that all are made in God's image and likeness

WAYS OF TURNING AWAY FROM HAPPINESS

MURDER: Have I taken the life of another or been involved in taking the life of another (including abortion)?

THEFT OR ROBBERY: Have I taken what belongs to another, either in secret or publicly?

RESTITUTION: Have I returned to others what I have borrowed or taken from them?

GOSSIP/CALUMNY: Have I disparaged someone's character? Have I accused someone wrongly? Have I caused emotional harm to another by word or deed (e.g. backbiting, gossiping, cursing, or cheating another)?

GOSSIP/DETRACTION: Have I harmed another's good reputation by revealing a truth which should not be told?

SUPERSTITION/THE OCCULT: Have I indulged in superstitious practices or have I used sacred objects in a superstitious way? Have I indulged in horoscopes, tarot cards, Ouija boards, etc.?

DEFAMATION: Have I publicly damaged the character of another through social media?

BODILY MUTILATION: Have I intentionally harmed my body through excessive piercings, tattoos, cutting, starvation, etc.?

IRRELIGION: Have I tried to tempt God's power? Perjured myself under oath? Misused or violated that which is sacred (sacrilege)?

DISOBEDIENCE: Have I willfully disobeyed a command from someone in authority over me? Have I held in contempt that authority or his command?

INGRATITUDE: Have I failed to express thanks for a favor received or failed to notice a favor received?

LYING: Have I intentionally told a falsehood? Have I lied with malicious intent (e.g. to make fun of others, to profit from the lie, etc.)?

DISSIMULATION/HYPOCRISY: Have I acted in such a way to portray myself as someone I am not? Have I behaved in a way that makes me seem like I am better, holier or wiser than I truly am?

COVETOUSNESS: Do I have an inordinate desire for wealth or possessions? Do I desire the goods of others?

PRODIGALITY: Do I spend money needlessly or excessively?

ACTING WITH PRUDENCE

PRUDENCE: Enables one to reason and to act rightly in any given situation — "right reason in action"

GIFT OF COUNSEL: Enables one to respond fully to direction and guidance from the Lord

CIRCUMSPECTION: Careful consideration of circumstances and consequences

DOCILITY: Willingness to be taught

FORESIGHT: Considering the consequences of one's actions; thinking ahead

WAYS OF TURNING AWAY FROM HAPPINESS

IMPRUDENCE: Have I engaged in risky behavior endangering my soul/well-being or that of others? Have I been thoughtless in my speech or actions?

NEGLIGENCE: Have I neglected my responsibilities as a child of God, spouse, parent or employee?

CARNAL "PRUDENCE": Have I seen carnal/material goods as more important than anything else? Have I been crafty, manipulative or fraudulent in my dealings with others?

Have I utilized integral parts of prudence while making decisions (memory, insight, docility, sagacity (reasonableness), reason, foresight, circumspection, caution)? Have I hastily acted on an impulse or procrastinated through indecisiveness?

CONTENDING
WITH FORTITUDE

FORTITUDE: Enables one to endure difficulties and pain for the sake of what is good

GIFT OF FORTITUDE: Moves one to endure difficulties for the sake of eternal life with God

MAGNANIMITY: Seeking with confidence to do great things in God, literally "having a large soul"

PERSEVERANCE: Taking steps necessary to carry out objectives in spite of difficulties

PATIENCE: Bearing present difficulties calmly

WAYS OF TURNING AWAY FROM HAPPINESS

COWARDICE: Do I fail to be virtuous out of inordinate fear?

FOOLHARDINESS: Have I placed myself in danger unnecessarily, out of pride? Do I text message while driving?

PRESUMPTION/VAINGLORY: Have I committed sin presuming God's forgiveness? Have I relied solely on my own capabilities as sufficient to handle anything?

FAINTHEARTEDNESS: Do I take on only what I can handle? Do I refuse to do what I can in a difficult situation, even though it is something I could well handle/overcome?

MEANNESS/LITTLENESS: Do I aspire to do only little things when greater things should be attempted?

NOTES:

_____

_____

_____

_____

_____

_____

MASTERING WITH TEMPERANCE

TEMPERANCE: Enables one to be moderate in the pleasure and use of created goods

GIFT OF FEAR OF THE LORD: Brings forth the fear of offending God by sin

MODERATION: Attention to balance in one's life

MODESTY: Purity of heart in action, especially in regards to dress and speech

ORDERLINESS: Keeping oneself physically clean and neat and one's belongings in good order

SELF-CONTROL: Joyful mastery over one's passions and desires

WAYS OF TURNING AWAY FROM HAPPINESS

GLUTTONY: Do I eat or drink excessively? Am I attached to fine foods or drink?

LUST: Have I freely entertained pornographic images on the internet, TV, magazines, etc? Have I entertained impure thoughts?

UNCHASTITY/IMPURITY: Have I abused my own sexuality, e.g., masturbation? Have I acted unchastely with others, e.g., engaged in pre-marital sexual relations or had an affair with someone who is married? Have I been unduly intimate with another person, whether the opposite or the same sex?

ANGER: Has my anger caused me to fight (physically or verbally) with another? Have I sought revenge as a result of a wrong because of inordinate anger?

CURIOSITY: Have I spent time studying things that are sinful/not useful? Do I spend an inordinate amount of time on the internet/texting?

IMMODESTY: Have I been immodest in my dress/behavior/speech?

NOTES:

HOW TO PRAY THE ROSARY

Praying the Rosary or 'the epitome of the whole Gospel' is another means of pondering, with Mary, the life of Christ.

1. MAKE THE SIGN OF THE CROSS AND PRAY THE APOSTLES' CREED

   I believe in God, the Father Almighty, Creator of heaven and earth; and in Jesus Christ, His only Son, our Lord, Who was conceived by the Holy Spirit, born of the Virgin Mary; suffered under Pontius Pilate, was crucified, died and was buried. He descended into hell; the third day He rose again from the dead; He ascended into heaven, is seated at the right hand of God the Father Almighty; from there He will come to judge the living and the dead. I believe in the Holy Spirit, the Holy Catholic Church, the communion of Saints, the forgiveness of sins, the resurrection of the body, and life everlasting. Amen.

2. PRAY THE OUR FATHER

   Our Father, who art in Heaven, hallowed be Thy name.
   Thy Kingdom come, Thy will be done, on earth as it is in heaven.
   Give us this day our daily bread, and forgive us our trespasses,
   as we forgive those who trespass against us.
   And lead us not into temptation, but deliver us from evil. Amen.

3. PRAY THREE HAIL MARY'S

   Hail Mary, full of Grace; the Lord is with thee.
   Blessed art thou among women,
   and blessed is the fruit of thy womb, Jesus.
   Holy Mary, Mother of God,
   pray for us sinners,
   now and at the hour of our death. Amen.

4. Pray the Glory Be

   Glory be to the Father, and to the Son, and to the Holy Spirit; as it was in the beginning, is now, and ever shall be, world without end. Amen.

5. ANNOUNCE THE FIRST MYSTERY AND PRAY THE OUR FATHER.

6. PRAY TEN HAIL MARY'S (WHILE MEDITATING ON THE MYSTERY).

7. PRAY THE GLORY BE.

8. RECITE "O MY JESUS."

   O my Jesus, forgive us our sins, save us from the fire of hell, lead all souls to Heaven, especially those in most need of Thy mercy.

9. ANNOUNCE THE SECOND MYSTERY AND PRAY THE OUR FATHER.
   (CONTINUE WITH THE 3RD, 4TH, AND 5TH MYSTERIES IN THE SAME WAY)

10. AFTER COMPLETING THE 5TH MYSTERY, PRAY THE SALVE REGINA OR HAIL HOLY QUEEN.

HAIL HOLY QUEEN

Hail, holy Queen, Mother of Mercy! Our life, our sweetness, and our hope! To thee do we cry, poor banished children of Eve. To thee do we send up our sighs, mourning and weeping in this valley of tears. Turn then, most gracious advocate, thine eyes of mercy toward us, and after this, our exile, show unto us the blessed fruit of thy womb, Jesus. O clement, o loving, o sweet Virgin Mary.

Pray for us, O holy Mother of God, that we may be made worthy of the promises of Christ.

THE MYSTERIES OF THE ROSARY

The Five Joyful Mysteries
1. The Annunciation (Lk. 1:26-38)
2. The Visitation (Lk. 1:40-42)
3. The Nativity (Lk. 2:8-7, Mt. 1)
4. The Presentation (Lk. 2:22-35)
5. The Finding of Jesus in the Temple (Lk. 2:41–52)

The Five Luminous Mysteries
1. The Baptism in the Jordan (Mt. 3:13-17)
2. The Wedding at Cana (Jn. 2:1-2)
3. The Proclamation of the Kingdom (Lk. 7:48-49)
4. The Transfiguration (Mt. 17:1-8)
5. The Institution of the Eucharist (Mt. 26:26-28)

The Five Sorrowful Mysteries
1. The Agony in the Garden (Lk. 22:39-46)
2. The Scourging at the Pillar (Mt. 27:26)
3. The Crowning with Thorns (Mk. 15:20-21)
4. The Carrying of the Cross (Lk. 23:26-32, Jn. 19:16-22)
5. The Crucifixion (Jn. 19:25-30)

The Five Glorious Mysteries
1. The Resurrection (Jn. 20:1-9)
2. The Ascension (Acts 1:9-11)
3. Pentecost (Acts 1:13-14, 2:1-4)
4. The Assumption (Lk. 1:46-49)
5. The Coronation (Rev. 11:19-12:1)

THE LITANY OF THE MOST PRECIOUS BLOOD OF JESUS

Lord, have mercy.	*Lord, have mercy*
Christ, have mercy.	*Christ, have mercy on us.*
Lord, have mercy.	*Lord, have mercy*
Jesus, hear us.	*Jesus, graciously hear us.*
God, the Father of Heaven,	*Have mercy on us.*
God, the Son, Redeemer of the world,	*Have mercy on us.*
God, the Holy Spirit,	*Have mercy on us.*
Holy Trinity, One God,	*Have mercy on us.*

Blood of Christ, only-begotten Son of the Eternal Father, *Save us.*
Blood of Christ, Incarnate Word of God, *Save us.*
Blood of Christ, of the New and Eternal Testament, *Save us.*
Blood of Christ, falling upon the earth in the Agony, *Save us.*
Blood of Christ, shed profusely in the Scourging, *Save us.*
Blood of Christ, flowing forth in the Crowning with Thorns, *Save us.*
Blood of Christ, poured out on the Cross, *Save us.*
Blood of Christ, price of our salvation, *Save us.*
Blood of Christ, without which there is no forgiveness. *Save us.*
Blood of Christ, Eucharistic drink and refreshment of souls, *Save us.*
Blood of Christ, stream of mercy, *Save us.*
Blood of Christ, victor over demons, *Save us.*
Blood of Christ, courage of Martyrs, *Save us.*
Blood of Christ, strength of Confessors, *Save us.*
Blood of Christ, bringing forth Virgins, *Save us.*
Blood of Christ, help of those in peril, *Save us.*
Blood of Christ, relief of the burdened, *Save us.*
Blood of Christ, solace in sorrow, *Save us.*
Blood of Christ, hope of the penitent, *Save us.*
Blood of Christ, consolation of the dying, *Save us.*
Blood of Christ, peace and tenderness of hearts, *Save us.*
Blood of Christ, pledge of eternal life, *Save us.*
Blood of Christ, freeing souls from purgatory, *Save us.*
Blood of Christ, most worthy of all glory and honor, *Save us.*

Lamb of God, who take away the sins of the world. *Spare us, O Lord*
Lamb of God, who take away the sins of the world, *Graciously hear us, O Lord.*
Lamb of God, who take away the sins of the world, *Have mercy on us.*

V. You have redeemed us, O Lord, in your Blood.
R. And made us, for our God, a kingdom.

Let us pray: Almighty and eternal God, you have appointed your only-begotten Son the Redeemer of the world, and willed to be appeased by his Blood. Grant we beg of you, that we may worthily adore this price of our salvation, and through its power be safeguarded from the evils of the present life, so that we may rejoice in its fruits forever in heaven. Through the same Christ our Lord. Amen.

ANIMA CHRISTI

Soul of Christ, sanctify me.
Body of Christ, save me.
Blood of Christ, inebriate me.
Water from the side of Christ, wash me.
Passion of Christ, strengthen me.
O Good Jesus, hear me.
Within your wounds hide me.
Permit me not to be separated from you.
From the wicked foe, defend me.
At the hour of my death, call me
And bid me come to you,
That with your saints
I may praise you forever and ever. Amen.

TO GOD THE HOLY SPIRIT

Come, O Spirit of Fortitude, and give fortitude to our souls. Make our hearts strong in all trials and in all distress, pouring forth abundantly into them the gifts of strength, that we may be able to resist the attacks of the devil.

Come, Holy Spirit! Drive far away from us our foes from hell, and grant us Your peace. Through all perils guide us safely. Amen.

MEMORARE TO OUR LADY

REMEMBER, O most gracious Virgin Mary, that never was it known that anyone who fled to thy protection, implored thy help, or sought thy intercession was left unaided. Inspired with this confidence, I fly to thee, O Virgin of virgins, my Mother; to thee do I come; before thee I stand, sinful and sorrowful. O Mother of the Word Incarnate, despise not my petitions, but in thy mercy hear and answer me. Amen.

CHAPLET OF DIVINE MERCY

1. MAKE THE SIGN OF THE CROSS AND PRAY ONE OUR FATHER

   Our Father, who art in Heaven, hallowed be Thy name.
   Thy Kingdom come, Thy will be done, on earth as it is in heaven. Give us this day our daily
   bread, and forgive us our trespasses, as we forgive those who trespass against us.
   And lead us not into temptation, but deliver us from evil. Amen.

2. PRAY ONE HAIL MARY

   Hail Mary, full of Grace; the Lord is with thee. Blessed art thou among women, and blessed
   is the fruit of thy womb, Jesus.
   Holy Mary, Mother of God, pray for us sinners, now and at the hour of our death. Amen.

3. PRAY THE APOSTLES' CREED

   I believe in God, the Father Almighty,
   Creator of heaven and earth;
   and in Jesus Christ, His only Son, our Lord,
   Who was conceived by the Holy Spirit,
   born of the Virgin Mary;
   suffered under Pontius Pilate,
   was crucified, died and was buried.
   He descended into hell;
   the third day He rose again from the dead;
   He ascended into heaven,
   is seated at the right hand of God the Father Almighty;
   from there He will come to judge the living and the dead.
   I believe in the Holy Spirit, the Holy Catholic Church,
   the communion of Saints, the forgiveness of sins,
   the resurrection of the body, and life everlasting.
   Amen.

Jesus I Trust in You!

4. TO START EACH DECADE, PRAY THE ETERNAL FATHER

   Eternal Father, I offer you the Body and Blood, Soul and Divinity, of your dearly Beloved
   Son, our Lord, Jesus Christ, in atonement for our sins, and those of the whole world.

5. ON THE TEN SMALL BEADS, PRAY:

   For the sake of His sorrowful Passion, have mercy on us, and on the whole world.

6. REPEAT STEPS FOUR AND FIVE FOR EACH DECADE. AFTER COMPLETING
   THE FIFTH DECADE, PRAY THREE TIMES:

   Holy God, Holy Mighty One, Holy Immortal One, have mercy on us, and on the whole world.

RENEWAL OF BAPTISMAL PROMISES

O Lord, my God, this day I renew my baptismal vows: I renounce sin, so that I can live in freedom as a child of God. I renounce the snares of the devil, so that sin cannot enslave me. I renounce Satan and all his works and all his pomps. I take Jesus Christ for my Deliverer and my Champion, my Model and my Guide. I promise to serve Him faithfully, whatever the cost, to the end of my life so that I can share in His everlasting triumph. Amen

ST. FRANCIS PRAYER BEFORE THE CRUCIFIX

O Most High and glorious God, enlighten the darkness of my heart. Give me, Lord, a firm faith, sure hope, and perfect love, profound humility—the sign and knowledge so that I may carry out all Your commandments. Amen.

O crux, ave, spes unica.
Hail, O Cross, our only hope!

PRAYER TO SAINT MICHAEL

Saint Michael the Archangel, defend us in battle, be our protection against the malice and snares of the devil. May God rebuke him we humbly pray; and do thou, O Prince of the Heavenly host, by the power of God, thrust into hell Satan and all evil spirits who wander through the world for the ruin of souls. Amen.

IN BAPTISM WE ARE GRAFTED ONTO CHRIST THE VINE;

He enters us and remains in us as long as we desire His presence. By freely choosing to live as one with Christ, we permit Him to transform us from within. This life in Christ is rooted in the virtues and gifts received at Baptism (*CCC* 1266).

If faith is like the root, charity is like the sap that nourishes the trunk and rises into the branches, the network of virtues, to produce the delicious fruit of good works." (Servais Pinckaers, O.P., Morality: The Catholic View, South Bend, St. Augustine Press, 2001)

The Disciple of Christ Virtues will guide you in identifying virtues which need to be cultivated. Each corresponding "Opposing Trait" highlights a pattern of behavior which needs change in order for you to mature in virtue.

Human virtues acquired by education, by deliberate acts, and by perseverance ever-renewed in repeated efforts are purified and elevated by divine grace. With God's help, they forge character and give facility in the practice of the good. The virtuous man is happy to practice them (*CCC*, 1810).

"GOD CAUSES THE GROWTH"
(1 CORINTHIANS 3:7)

VIRTUE	MEANING	OPPOSING TRAIT
JUSTICE (Fairness)	Enables one to give to each what is due to him, beginning with God	Failing to see what is owed to each by virtue of his dignity
AFFABILITY	Being easy to approach and talk to	Being mean, unkind, cruel, or unflattering
COURTESY	Treating other people with respect, recognizing that all are made in God's image and likeness	Not recognizing the inherent dignity of others made in God's image
GENEROSITY	Giving of oneself in a willing and cheerful manner for the good of others	Giving without a spirit of cheer, with a begrudging manner
GRATITUDE	Thankful disposition of mind and heart	Not expressing appreciation; taking other people and things for granted
KINDNESS	Expressing genuine concern about the well-being of others; anticipating their needs	Not regarding the well-being of others, being cruel in looks, words, and actions
LOYALTY	Accepting the bonds implicit in relationships and defending the virtues upheld by Church, family, and country	Breaking bonds of trust with Church, family, country, friends, and school
OBEDIENCE	Assenting to rightful authority without hesitation or resistance	Resisting the directives of rightful authority
PATRIOTISM	Paying due honor and respect to our country, with a willingness to serve	Lacking regard or respect for one's country and national symbols
PRAYERFULNESS	Being still, listening, and willing to talk to God as a friend	Entertaining distractions during prayers and Mass
RESPECT	Speaking and acting according to our own and others' rights, status, and circumstances	Resisting the directives of rightful authority
RESPONSIBILITY	Fulfilling our just duties; accepting the consequences of our words and actions, intentional and unintentional	Failing to accept responsibility for one's words and/or actions; being unreliable
SINCERITY	Trustfulness in words and actions; honesty and enthusiasm towards others	Speaking or acting in a manner only to make oneself look good; being insincere
TRUSTWORTHINESS	Acting in a way that inspires confidence and trust; being reliable	Being devious or deceptive

 SELECT A VIRTUE YOU NEED TO PRACTICE.

VIRTUE	MEANING	OPPOSING TRAIT
PRUDENCE Sound Judgment	Enables one to reason and to act rightly in any given situation – "right reason in action"	Being hasty or rash in one's words or actions
PARTS OF A PRUDENTIAL ACT		
GOOD COUNSEL Ask and listen	Seeking advice from a reasonable person	Seeking advice from those who agree with you; Asking moral advice from people who do not share your moral values
GOOD JUDGMENT Think	Thinking rightly about a decision	Acting without thinking
COMMAND Act	Directly acting upon a sound decision	Failing to act upon a sound decision
VIRTUES		
CIRCUMSPECTION	Careful consideration of circumstances and consequences	Considering only oneself when acting
DOCILITY	Willingness to be taught	Being stubborn, inflexible, and proudly set in one's ways
FORESIGHT	Consideration of the consequences of one's actions, thinking ahead	Failing to consider later consequences

SELECT A VIRTUE YOU NEED TO PRACTICE.

_____

_____

_____

_____

VIRTUE	MEANING	OPPOSING TRAIT
FORTITUDE (Courage)	Enables one to endure difficulties and pain for the sake of what is good	Choosing the easiest task; being cowardly; being insensible to fear
INDUSTRIOUSNESS	Diligence, especially in work that leads to natural and supernatural maturity	Giving in to a lack of motivation to complete one's responsibilities; being lazy
MAGNANIMITY	Seeking with confidence to do great things in God; literally "having a large soul"	Seeking to do great things for self-promotion ; not seeking to do the good that is possible – pusillanimity (weak, spineless)
MAGNIFICENCE	Doing great things for God	Being wasteful; not responding to grace
PATIENCE	Bearing present difficulties calmly	Being impatient while completing a difficult task or in handling challenging circumstances
PERSEVERANCE	Taking the steps necessary to carry out objectives in spite of difficulties	Quickly giving up when a task is challenging
TEMPERANCE (Self-Control)	Enables one to be moderate in the pleasure and use of created goods	Intemperance; overindulging in a good thing
HONESTY	Sincerity, openness and truthfulness in one's words and actions	Being dishonest in words and actions; telling lies
HUMILITY	Awareness that all our gifts come from God and appreciation for the gifts of others	Failing to recognize the gifts of others; being too proud or having false humility.
MEEKNESS	Serenity of spirit while focusing on the needs of others	Giving in to anger and losing one's temper when working or playing with others
MODERATION	Attention to balance in one's life	Giving in to being excessive in one or more areas of one's life
MODESTY	Purity of heart in action, especially in regards to dress and speech	Choosing to dress or act in a way inconsistent with one's dignity as a child of God
ORDERLINESS	Keeping ourselves physical appearance clean and neat and our belongings in good order	Disorder with regard to one's space and physical appearance
SELF-CONTROL	Joyful mastery over our passions and desires	Being excessive in words or actions, acting impulsively

 SELECT A VIRTUE YOU NEED TO PRACTICE.

_____

_____

_____

_____

CORPORAL WORKS OF MERCY

† **GIVE FOOD TO THE HUNGRY:** Making a personal sacrifice to nourish another person's body and soul

† **GIVE DRINK TO THE THIRSTY:** Giving others refreshment to sustain their physical and spiritual life

† **CLOTHE THE NAKED:** Aiding others in recognizing the dignity of their bodies by treating them in a manner that expresses this dignity

† **SHELTER THE HOMELESS:** Welcoming others and making them feel at home; giving them an experience of kindness and security

† **VISIT THE SICK:** Supporting those bearing Christ's Cross with your prayer and presence

† **VISIT THE IMPRISONED:** Reaching out through prayer and kind support to those in prison or who have less freedom

† **BURY THE DEAD:** Laying to rest the body of someone who has died and helping their loved ones grieve

SPIRITUAL WORKS OF MERCY

† **TEACHING THE IGNORANT:** Teaching others the knowledge they need to be happy and fulfilled in this life and in the next

† **COUNSEL THE DOUBTFUL:** Bringing peace of mind to another through good advice and uplifting words and deeds

† **ADMONISH THE SINNER:** Calling others to conversion and encouraging them in pursuit of holiness

† **BEAR WRONGS PATIENTLY:** Receiving slights, insults, and inconveniences cheerfully and without judging or expressing irritation

† **FORGIVE OFFENSES:** Extending God's merciful love to someone who has hurt you, and letting go of his or her guilt

† **COMFORT THE SORROWFUL:** Lightening another's burden of sorrow through care and compassion

† **PRAY FOR THE LIVING & THE DEAD:** Loving your neighbor as yourself through interceding for the needs of all

"WHAT GOOD IS IT, MY BROTHERS, IF SOMEONE SAYS HE HAS FAITH BUT DOES NOT HAVE WORKS? CAN THAT FAITH SAVE HIM? IF A BROTHER OR SISTER HAS NOTHING TO WEAR AND HAS NO FOOD FOR THE DAY, AND ONE OF YOU SAYS TO THEM, "GO IN PEACE, KEEP WARM, AND EAT WELL," BUT YOU DO NOT GIVE THEM THE NECESSITIES OF THE BODY, WHAT GOOD IS IT? SO ALSO FAITH OF ITSELF, IF IT DOES NOT HAVE WORKS, IS DEAD." *—James 2:14-17*

"God is love" (1 John 4:8), and so everything that He does is rooted in the foundation of His love. Your existence is rooted in His love. To be a disciple of Christ means to live, ever more deeply, in the mystery of God's love for you personally. His love is the foundation of your life, of your identity, of your being. His love is what is my sure support, "my refuge, my fortress, my God in whom I trust" (Psalm 91:1).

When His love is the foundation of your identity and worth, you are free to love Him in return. To be a disciple of Christ means to love God above all things and your neighbor as yourself. Practicing the works of mercy is a concrete way to show your love of God and neighbor.

NOTES:

_____

_____

_____

_____

_____

_____

_____

_____

_____

_____

_____

O LORD. I WANT TO BE COMPLETELY TRANSFORMED INTO YOUR MERCY AND TO BE YOUR LIVING REFLECTION. MAY THE GREATEST OF ALL DIVINE ATTRIBUTES, THAT OF YOUR UNFATHOMABLE MERCY, PASS THROUGH MY HEART AND SOUL TO MY NEIGHBOR.

HELP ME, O LORD, *THAT MY EYES MAY BE MERCIFUL,* SO THAT I MAY NEVER SUSPECT OR JUDGE FROM APPEARANCES, BUT LOOK FOR WHAT IS BEAUTIFUL IN MY NEIGHBORS' SOULS AND COME TO THEIR RESCUE.

HELP ME, O LORD, *THAT MY EARS MAY BE MERCIFUL,* SO THAT I MAY GIVE HEED TO MY NEIGHBORS' NEEDS AND NOT BE INDIFFERENT TO THEIR PAINS AND MOANINGS.

HELP ME, O LORD, *THAT MY TONGUE MAY BE MERCIFUL,* SO THAT I SHOULD NEVER SPEAK NEGATIVELY OF MY NEIGHBOR, BUT HAVE A WORD OF COMFORT AND FORGIVENESS FOR ALL.

HELP ME, O LORD, *THAT MY HANDS MAY BE MERCIFUL* AND FILLED WITH GOOD DEEDS, SO THAT I MAY DO ONLY GOOD TO MY NEIGHBORS AND TAKE UPON MYSELF THE MORE DIFFICULT AND TOILSOME TASKS.

HELP ME, O LORD, *THAT MY FEET MAY BE MERCIFUL,* SO THAT I MAY HURRY TO ASSIST MY NEIGHBOR, OVERCOMING MY OWN FATIGUE AND WEARINESS. MY TRUE REST IS IN THE SERVICE OF MY NEIGHBOR.

HELP ME, O LORD, *THAT MY HEART MAY BE MERCIFUL* SO THAT I MYSELF MAY FEEL ALL THE SUFFERINGS OF MY NEIGHBOR. I WILL REFUSE MY HEART TO NO ONE. I WILL BE SINCERE EVEN WITH THOSE WHO I KNOW WILL ABUSE MY KINDNESS. I WILL BEAR MY OWN SUFFERING IN SILENCE. MAY YOUR MERCY REST UPON ME.

O MY JESUS, TRANSFORM ME IN YOURSELF, FOR YOU CAN DO ALL THINGS.

- ST. MARIA FAUSTINA KOWALSKA

VIRTUE CHALLENGE: We *CHALLENGE YOU* to incorporate the Works of Mercy into your daily life.

LEARN–LIVE–WITNESS

HOW CAN YOU BE A WITNESS OF GOD'S LOVE AND TENDERNESS TO "ONE OF THESE LEAST BROTHERS OF MINE?" MATTHEW 25:40

 Learn to listen to God through prayer and reading His Word. Ask God how he may use you to be a witness to others.

 LIVE the virtues in your every day life.

 SERVE others by incorporating the Works of Mercy into your life.

NOTES:

_____
_____
_____
_____
_____
_____
_____
_____
_____
_____

Credits

Cover Artwork: *Mother of Life*, 2011, Nellie Edwards / paintedfaith.net

Page 4: *The Virgin and Child Embracing*, Sassoferrato, II (Biovanni Battista Salvi) / National Gallery, London, UK / Bridgeman Images

Page 9 : *Our Lady Worshipping the Child*, Correggio, (Antonio Allegri) / Galleria degli Uffizi, Florence, Italy / Bridgeman Images

Page 15: *The Miracle of the Loaves and Fishes*, illustration for 'The Life of Christ', Tissot, James Jacques Joseph / Brooklyn Museum of Art, New York, USA/ Bridgeman Images

Page 17: *Madonna and Child*, Sassoferrato, Il (Giovanni Battista Salvi) / Palazzo Ducale, Urbino, Italy / Bridgeman Images

Page 21: *Feed My Lambs, illustration for 'The Life of Christ'*, Tissot, James Jacques Joseph / Brooklyn Museum of Art, New York, USA / Bridgeman Images

Page 23: *Annunciation*, 1587, by Scipione Pulzone, oil on canvas, / De Agostini Picture Library / A. Dagli Orti / Bridgeman Images

Page 25: *The Palsied Man Let Down Through the Roof,* illustration for The Life of Christ, Tissot, James Jacques Joseph / Brooklyn Museum of Art, New York, USA / Bridgeman Images

Page 27: *Infant Jesus with the Lamb, Luini*, Bernardino / Pinacoteca Ambrosiana, Milan, Italy / De Agostini Picture Library / G. Cigolini / © Veneranda Biblioteca Ambrosiana – Milano / Bridgeman Images

Page 29: *The Life of Christ,* w, James Jacques Joseph / Brooklyn Museum of Art, New York, USA / Purchased by Public Subscription / Bridgeman Images

Page 35: *Jesus Discourses with His Disciples, illustration from 'The Life of Our Lord Jesus Christ'*, Tissot, James Jacques Joseph (1836-1902) / Brooklyn Museum of Art, New York, USA / Purchased by Public Subscription / Bridgeman Images

Page 43: *Jesus Heals the Blind and Lame on the Mountain*, illustration from 'The Life of Our Lord Jesus Christ' (w/c over graphite on paper), Tissot, James Jacques Joseph (1836-1902) / Brooklyn Museum of Art, New York, USA / Bridgeman Images

Page 49: *An Angel Announcing to the Shepherds of Bethlehem the Birth of Jesus.* The Life of Jesus of Nazareth by William Hole (Eyre and Spottiswoode, c 1905), UIG / Bridgeman Images

Page 53: *The Dream of St. Joseph*, Giordano, Luca / Indianapolis Museum of Art, USA / Martha Delzell Memorial Fund / Bridgeman Images

Page 57: *The Annunciation*, 17th century, Murillo, Bartolome Esteban / Prado, Madrid, Spain / Bridgeman Images

Page 59: *Visitation, from the Predella of the Annunciation Alterpiece*, Angelico, Fra (Guido di Pietro) / Prado, Madrid, Spain / Bridgeman Images

Page 61: *The Virgin Annunciate*, Batoni, Pompeo Girolamo / Private Collection / Photo © Bonhams, London, UK / Bridgeman Images

Page 63: *The Naming of John The Baptist*, Gothic Art. Flanders. Rogier van der Weyden or Roger de la Pature. Early Flemish painter. Gemaldegaterie, Berlin / Photo © Tarker / Bridgeman Images

Page 65: *The Holy Family with the infant St. John*, Murillo, Bartolome Esteban © Belvoir Castle, Leicestershire, UK / Bridgeman Images

Page 67: *Adoration of the Baby*, Honthorst, Gerrit van / Galleria degli Uffizi, Florence, Italy / Bridgeman Images

Page 69: *The Adoration of the Child with St. John the Baptist and St. Romauld of Ravenna* c.1463 (tempera on panel), Lippi, Fra Filippo (c.1406-69) / Galleria degli Uffizi, Florence, Italy / Bridgeman Images

Page 71: *The Immaculate Conception,*Tiepolo, Giovanni Battista (Giambattista) / Prado, Madrid, Spain / Photo © AISA / Bridgeman Images

Page 79: *Return of the Prodigal Son*, 1773 (oil on canvas), Batoni, Pompeo Girolamo (1708-87) / Kunsthistorisches Museum, Vienna, Austria / Bridgeman Images

Page 83: *Christ and the Rich Young Ruler,* 1889, Heinrich Hoffman, Public Domain

Page 88: *The Crucifixion* (fresco), Giotto di Bondone (c.1266-1337) / San Francesco, Lower Church, Assisi, Italy / Alinari / Bridgeman Images

Page 91: *Saint Michael banishes the devil to the abyss*, 1665/68, Murillo, Bartolome Esteban (1618-82) / Kunsthistorisches Museum, Vienna, Austria / Bridgeman Images

IF YOU LIKED OUR ADVENT JOURNAL,
you may like the following journals:

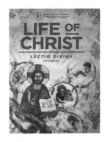

The Life of Christ Lectio Divina Journal was written to allow you to have an encounter with the Person of Jesus Christ. As you journey through the life of Christ by reading the selected scripture passages, you will slowly move through His life, meditating upon His word using *lectio divina*. This encounter with Truth, Beauty, and Goodness, will show you how a life of virtue becomes an interior habit, a way of life, which enables you to be more open to the Holy Spirit, allowing you to make your own personal commitment to live as a disciple of Christ.

Includes over 75 religious art images! Recommended for junior high, high school students and adults! **$21.95 | 326 p. | www.educationinvirtue.com**

This *lectio divina* journal has a 12-week cycle which focuses on one Scripture passage each week. Focusing on the spiritual and corporal works of mercy, the reader will respond to guided questions, religious artwork, selected readings and the challenge to "see" others doing works of mercy as well as performing them. Recommended for junior high, high school students and adults! **$11.95 | 140 p. | www.educationinvirtue.com**

Disciple of Christ-Education in Virtue® presents the Lenten Journal to help individuals use the liturgical season as a time of discipline and growth, or 'conditioning' that they might grow closer to the Person of Jesus Christ. After praying for the gift of self-knowledge to recognize an area of their heart which needs 'conditioning', the reader will be able to open their mind and heart to the Holy Spirit and encounter the word of God using *lectio divina* as well as give praise to Him using the gratitude log. The journal also allows for meditation by providing beautiful images of the Stations of the Cross.
$11.95 | www.educationinvirtue.com

VISIT WWW.EDUCATIONINVIRTUE.COM TO LEARN MORE.

Notes